PURPOSE in PRAYER

Purpose in Prayer

E. M. BOUNDS

Whitaker House

All Scripture quotations are from the *King James Version* (KJV) of the Bible.

PURPOSE IN PRAYER

ISBN: 0-88368-438-1
Printed in the United States of America
Copyright © 1997 by Whitaker House

Whitaker House
30 Hunt Valley Circle
New Kensington, PA 15068

3 4 5 6 7 8 9 10 11 12 / 06 05 04 03 02 01

Contents

Chapter 1

The Force That
Shapes the World

My creed leads me to think that prayer is efficacious, and surely a day's asking God to overrule all events for good is not lost.
—James Gilmour

The prayers of God's saints are the capital stock in heaven by which Christ carries on His great work upon the earth. Great throes and mighty convulsions in the world have come about as a result of these prayers. The earth is changed, revolutionized; angels move on more powerful, more rapid wings; and God's policy is shaped when the prayers of His people are more numerous and more efficient.

The most important lesson we can learn is how to pray. Indeed, we must pray so that our prayers take hold of God. The man who has done the most and the best praying is the most immortal, because prayers do not die. Perhaps the lips that uttered them are closed in death, or the heart that felt them may have ceased to beat, but the prayers live before God, and God's heart is set on them. Prayers outlive the lives of those who uttered them—outlive a generation, outlive an age, outlive a world.

Prayer is no fitful, short-lived thing. It is no voice crying unheard and unheeded in the silence. It is a voice that goes into God's ear, and it lives as long as God's ear is open to holy pleas, as long as God's heart is alive to holy things.

The mightiest successes that come to God's cause are created and carried on by prayer in God's day of power. When God's church comes into its mightiest inheritance of the mightiest faith and mightiest prayer, the angelic days of powerful activity occur. God's conquering days are when the saints have given themselves to mightiest prayer.

The life of the church is the highest life, and its office is to pray. Its prayer life is the highest life, the most fragrant, the most conspicuous. When God's house on the earth is a house of prayer, then God's house in heaven is busy and powerful in its plans and movements. "For mine house shall be called an house of prayer for all people" (Isa. 56:7), says our God.

Then, His earthly armies are clothed with the triumphs and spoils of victory, and His enemies are defeated on every hand.

God shapes the world by prayer. The more praying there is in the world, the better the world will be and the mightier the forces against evil everywhere. Prayer, in one phase of its operation, is a disinfectant and a preventive. It purifies the air; it destroys the contagion of evil.

The very life and prosperity of God's cause—even its very existence—depend on prayer. And the advance and triumph of His cause depend on one thing: that we ask of Him.

The Lord has issued His decree, immutable and eternal, in which we find the great condition of prayer:

> *I will declare the decree:...**Ask of me,**
> *and I shall give thee the heathen for*
> *thine inheritance, and the uttermost*
> *parts of the earth for thy possession.*
> *Thou shalt break them with a rod of*
> *iron; thou shalt dash them in pieces like*
> *a potter's vessel.*
> *(Ps. 2:7–9, emphasis added)*

Ask of Me. That is the condition—God desires a praying people, willing and obedient.

Under this universal and simple promise, men and women of old laid themselves out before God. They prayed, and God answered their prayers. Thus, the cause of God was kept alive in the world by the flame of their praying.

The second Psalm contains the divine description of the establishment of God's cause through Jesus Christ. All inferior dispensations have merged in the enthronement of Jesus Christ. In the following passage, God declares the enthronement of His Son:

> *Yet have I set my king upon my holy hill of Zion. I will declare the decree: the LORD hath said unto me, Thou art my Son; this day have I begotten thee.*
>
> *(Ps. 2:6–7)*

All the nations are incensed with bitter hatred against His cause, but God is described as laughing at their enfeebled hate:

> *Why do the heathen rage, and the people imagine a vain thing?....He that sitteth in the heavens shall laugh: the Lord shall have them in derision.* *(Ps. 2:1, 4)*

Prayer puts God in full force in the world. To a prayerful man, God is present in realized force. The man who has prayed many acceptable prayers has done the truest and greatest service to the incoming generation. To a prayerful church, God is present in glorious power. The prayers of God's saints strengthen the unborn generation against the desolating waves of sin and evil. Woe to the generation of sons who find their own censers empty of the rich incense of prayer, whose fathers have been too busy or too unbelieving to pray, and who have inexpressible perils and untold consequences for their heritage! They whose fathers and mothers have left them a wealthy legacy of prayer are very fortunate, indeed.

Prayer is God's settled and singular condition to move ahead His Son's kingdom. Therefore, the believer who is the most highly skilled in prayer will do the most for God. Men are to pray—to pray for the advance of God's cause. The one who can wield the power of prayer is the strong one, the holy one, in Christ's kingdom. He is one of God's heroes, God's saints, God's servants, God's agents. "Ask, and it shall be given you; seek, and ye shall find; knock, and it shall be opened unto you" (Matt. 7:7). The strongest one in Christ's kingdom is he who can knock the best, and the secret of success in Christ's kingdom is the ability to pray.

Chapter 2

The Fire That Consumes

The prayers of holy men appease God's wrath, drive away temptations, resist and overcome the Devil, procure the ministry and service of angels, rescind the decrees of God. Prayer cures sickness and obtains pardon; it arrests the sun in its course and stays the wheels of the chariot of the moon; it rules over all gods and opens and shuts the storehouses of rain; it unlocks the cabinet of the womb and quenches the violence of fire; it stops the mouths of lions and reconciles our suffering and weak faculties with the violence of torment and violence of persecution; it pleases God and supplies all our need.

—Jeremy Taylor

Prayer has an incredible power to arrest and change the purposes of God. The stroke of His power is relieved by the prayers of righteous men. We can witness both

the possibilities and the necessity of prayer
when we see how, in the following examples
from the Scriptures, the prayers of God's
saints brought about a change in God's plans.
Our first example of this is found in Genesis,
when Abimelech had been smitten by God:

> *So Abraham prayed unto God: and God
> healed Abimelech, and his wife, and his
> maidservants; and they bare children.
> For the LORD had fast closed up all the
> wombs of the house of Abimelech, be-
> cause of Sarah Abraham's wife.*
> *(Gen. 20:17–18)*

In another example, Job's miserable, mis-
taken comforters had so behaved themselves in
their controversy with Job that God's wrath
was kindled against them:

> *My servant Job shall pray for you: for
> him will I accept: lest I deal with you af-
> ter your folly, in that ye have not spoken
> of me the thing which is right, like my
> servant Job....And the LORD turned the
> captivity of Job, when he prayed for his
> friends.* *(Job 42:8, 10)*

When Jonah tried to run from the Lord, he
was in a dire condition. "The LORD sent out a

great wind into the sea, and there was a mighty tempest" (Jonah 1:4). When lots were cast among those aboard the ship, "the lot fell upon Jonah" (v. 7). He was cast overboard into the sea, but,

> *The LORD had prepared a great fish to swallow up Jonah....Then Jonah prayed unto the LORD his God out of the fish's belly, and said, I cried by reason of mine affliction unto the LORD, and he heard me; out of the belly of hell cried I, and thou heardest my voice....And the LORD spake unto the fish, and it vomited out Jonah upon the dry land.*
>
> *(Jonah 1:17–2:2, 10)*

Jonah prayed while imprisoned in the great fish; and when the disobedient prophet lifted up his voice in prayer, God heard him and sent deliverance. Thus Jonah came to dry land, saved from storm and sea and monsters of the deep, by the mighty energy of his praying.

It was the purpose of God to destroy the great and wicked city of Nineveh. "Yet forty days, and Nineveh shall be overthrown" (Jonah 3:4) was God's decree against the city. However, Nineveh prayed. Covered with sackcloth and sitting in ashes, she cried "mightily unto God" (v. 8). "And God repented of the evil, that he had said that he would do unto them; and he did it not" (v. 10).

Pharaoh was a firm believer in the possibilities of prayer and its ability to relieve. While staggering under the woeful curses of God, he pleaded with Moses to intercede for him. "Entreat the LORD for me" was his pathetic appeal, which he repeated four times (see Exodus 8:8, 28; 9:28; 10:17) when the plagues were scourging Egypt. Four times were these urgent appeals made to Moses, and four times did prayer lift the awful curse from the hard ruler and his doomed land.

The blasphemy and idolatry of Israel, in making the golden calf and declaring their devotion to it, were fearful crimes. The anger of God waxed hot, and He declared that He would destroy the offending people. The Lord was also extremely angry with Aaron. He said to Moses, "Let me alone, that I may destroy them" (Deut. 9:14). Undaunted, Moses prayed, and he kept on praying for forty days and nights. He recorded his prayer struggle in the ninth chapter of Deuteronomy:

> *And I fell down before the LORD, as at the first, forty days and forty nights: I did neither eat bread, nor drink water,*

*because of all your sins which ye sinned,
in doing wickedly in the sight of the
LORD, to provoke him to anger. For I
was afraid of the anger and hot displeasure, wherewith the LORD was wroth
against you to destroy you. But the LORD
hearkened unto me at that time also.
And the LORD was very angry with
Aaron to have destroyed him: and I
prayed for Aaron also the same time.*

(Deut. 9:18–20)

The message of God to Hezekiah was a
warning of death, as can be seen in this passage from Isaiah:

*Thus saith the LORD, Set thine house in
order: for thou shalt die, and not live.
Then Hezekiah turned his face toward
the wall, and prayed unto the LORD, and
said, Remember now, O LORD, I beseech
thee, how I have walked before thee in
truth and with a perfect heart, and have
done that which is good in thy sight.
And Hezekiah wept sore. Then came the
word of the LORD to Isaiah, saying, Go,
and say to Hezekiah, Thus saith the
LORD, the God of David thy father, I
have heard thy prayer, I have seen thy
tears: behold, I will add unto thy days
fifteen years.*   *(Isa. 38:1–5)*

Hezekiah's prayer changed God's purpose, and fifteen years were added to his life.

The Syrophenician woman (see Mark 7:24–30), the importunate[1] widow (see Luke 18:1–7), and the friend at midnight (see Luke 11:5–10) are wonderful lessons of what dauntless prayer can do in mastering or defying conditions, in changing defeat into victory and triumphing in the regions of despair.

All these people of God knew how to pray and how to prevail in prayer. Their faith in prayer was no passing attitude that changed with the wind or with their own feelings and circumstances; they were confident that God always heard and answered, that His ear was always open to the cry of His children, and that the power to do what was asked of Him was equal to His willingness. Thus, strong in faith and in prayer, they

> *subdued kingdoms, wrought righteousness, obtained promises, stopped the mouths of lions, quenched the violence of fire, escaped the edge of the sword, out of weakness were made strong, waxed valiant in fight, turned to flight the armies of the aliens.* (Heb. 11:33–34)

---

[1] Importunate: persistent in request or demand, to the point of being troublesome.

Everything was possible to the men and women who knew how to pray, and it is still possible today. Prayer, indeed, opened a limitless storehouse, and God's hand withheld nothing. Prayer introduced those who practiced it into a world of privilege, and brought the strength and wealth of heaven down to the aid of finite man. What rich and wonderful power they had who had learned the secret of victorious approach to God! With Moses it saved a nation; with Ezra it saved a church. (See Ezra 1:1–4 and Ezra 7–9.)

And yet, strange as it seems when we contemplate the wonders of which God's people had been witnesses, they became slack in prayer. The mighty hold upon God, which had so often struck awe and terror into the hearts of their enemies, lost its grip. The people, backslidden and apostate, had gone off from their praying—if the bulk of them had ever truly prayed. The Pharisee's cold and lifeless praying was substituted for any genuine approach to God, and because of that formal method of praying, the whole of their worship became a parody of its real purpose. The dispensation was glorious, and gloriously executed, by Moses, by Ezra, by Daniel and Elijah, by Hannah and Samuel; but the circle seemed limited and short-lived; the praying ones were few and far between. They had no survivors, none to imitate their devotion to God, none to preserve the roll of the elect.

In vain had the decree established the divine order, the divine call, *Ask of Me*. From their earnest and fruitful crying to God, the Israelites turned their faces to pagan gods and cried in vain for the answers that could never come. Thus, they sank into that godless and pitiful state in which they lost their purpose in life, because the link with the Eternal had been broken. Their favored dispensation of prayer was forgotten; they no longer knew how to pray.

What a contrast to the achievements that brighten up other pages of the Holy Scriptures! The power that worked through Elijah and Elisha, in answer to prayer, reached down even to the grave. Through both men, a child was raised from the dead (see 1 Kings 17:17–24; 2 Kings 4:18–37), and the powers of famine were broken. (See 1 Kings 18:1–2, 41–45; 2 Kings 4:38–44.) Note what James wrote about Elijah:

> *The effectual fervent prayer of a righteous man availeth much. Elias was a man subject to like passions as we are, and he prayed earnestly that it might not rain: and it rained not on the earth*

*by the space of three years and six
months. And he prayed again, and the
heaven gave rain, and the earth brought
forth her fruit.*   *(James 5:16–18)*

How wide is the provision of the grace of
praying, as administered in that marvelous
dispensation! The saints of old prayed won-
drously. Why could their praying not save the
era from decay and death? Was it not because
they had lost the fire without which all praying
degenerates into a lifeless form? It takes effort
and toil and care to prepare the incense.
Prayer is no laggard's work. When all the rich,
spiced graces from the body of prayer have
been blended and refined and intermixed by
labor and beating, the fire is needed to unloose
the incense and make its fragrance rise to the
throne of God. The spirit and life of the incense is created by the fire that consumes.
Without this fire, prayer has no spirit. Like
dead spices, it is for corruption and worms.

The casual, intermittent prayer is never
bathed in this divine fire. This haphazard way
of praying lacks the earnestness that lays hold
of God and is determined not to let Him go until the blessing comes. (See Genesis 32:26.)
"Pray without ceasing" (1 Thess. 5:17), counseled the great apostle. That is the habit that

drives prayer right into the mortar that holds
the building stones together. "You can do more
than pray after you have prayed," said the
godly Dr. A. J. Gordon,[2] "but you cannot do
more than pray until you have prayed." The
story of every great Christian achievement is
the history of answered prayer.

Alexander Whyte wrote:

> The greatest and the best talent
> that God gives to any man or woman in
> this world is the talent of prayer. And
> the best payment of interest that any
> man or woman brings back to God when
> He comes to reckon with them at the
> end of this world, is a life of prayer. And
> those servants best put their Lord's
> money "to the exchangers" (Matt.
> 25:27) who rise early and sit late, as
> long as they are in this world, ever
> finding out and ever following after bet-
> ter and better methods of prayer, and
> ever forming more secret, more stead-
> fast, and more spiritually fruitful habits
> of prayer, until they literally "pray
> without ceasing" (1 Thess. 5:17); and

---

[2] A. J. Gordon (1836–1895): Adoniram Judson Gordon, pastor of
Clarendon Street Church in Boston beginning in 1869. He
founded and led a missionary training school, and he undertook
a wide variety of evangelistic and social outreach.

until they continually strike out into new enterprises in prayer, and new achievements, and new enrichments.

When once asked what his plans for the following day were, Martin Luther answered: "Work, work, from early until late. In fact, I have so much to do that I shall spend the first three hours in prayer." Cromwell, too, believed in being much upon his knees. On one occasion, while looking at some statues of famous men, he turned to a friend and said: "Make mine kneeling, for thus I came to glory."

It is only when the whole heart is gripped with the passion of prayer that the life-giving fire descends, for none but the earnest man gets access to the ear of God; and that is the purpose of prayer.

Chapter 3

"Ask of Me"

We must remember that the goal of prayer is the ear of God. Unless that is gained, the prayer has utterly failed. The uttering of it may have kindled devotional feeling in our minds, the hearing of it may have comforted and strengthened the hearts of those with whom we have prayed, but if the prayer has not gained the heart of God, it has failed in its essential purpose.
—Charles Spurgeon

In prayer, man's access to God opens everything, and makes his impoverishment his wealth. We have seen how prayer changes the purposes of God, and stays or moves His mighty hand. All things are available to man through prayer. Man is given the privilege to command God, who has all this authority and power, in accordance with the demands of God's earthly kingdom. Look again at the passage in Psalm 2, beginning with verse eight:

Ask of me, and I shall give thee the hea-
then for thine inheritance, and the ut-
termost parts of the earth for thy
possession. Thou shalt break them with
a rod of iron; thou shalt dash them in
pieces like a potter's vessel.   (Ps. 2:8–9)

Heaven, with all that it has, is under obligation to carry out the ultimate, final, and glorious purposes of God. Why, then, is the time
so long in carrying out these wise benedictions
for man? Why, then, does sin reign so long?
Why are the oath-bound covenant promises so
long in coming to their gracious end? Sin
reigns, Satan reigns, sighing marks the lives of
many; all tears are fresh and full.

Why is all this so? Because we have not
prayed to bring the evil to an end; we have not
prayed as we must pray. We have not met the
conditions of prayer.

More praying, and better praying, is the
key to the whole matter. The more time we
spend in prayer, and the more preparations we
make to meet God, the more we will commune
with God through Christ. But our manner of
praying, and the things about which we pray,
are not entirely pleasing to God. Baptist phi-
losopher John Foster has said: "More and better praying will bring the surest and readiest

triumph to God's cause; feeble, formal, listless praying brings decay and death."

What, then, are we to do? We must prepare ourselves to pray, to be like Christ, and to pray like Christ. We must meet the conditions of prayer. We can begin to examine the conditions of prayer by reading these verses from Isaiah:

> *Thus saith the LORD, the Holy One of Israel, and his Maker, Ask me of things to come concerning my sons, and concerning the work of my hands command ye me. I have made the earth, and created man upon it: I, even my hands, have stretched out the heavens, and all their host have I commanded. (Isa. 45:11–12)*

Ask of Me. Ask of God. We have not rested on prayer. We have not made prayer the sole condition. There has been a violation of the primary condition of prayer. We have not prayed correctly. We have not prayed at all. God is willing to give, but we are slow to ask. The Son, through His saints, is ever praying (see Hebrews 7:25), and God the Father is ever answering.

Ask of Me. In the invitation is conveyed the assurance of an answer; the shout of victory is there and may be heard by the listening ear. The Father holds the authority and power in His hands. How easy is the condition, and yet how slow we are in fulfilling the condition! Nations are in bondage; the uttermost parts of the earth are still not possessed. The earth groans (see Romans 8:22); the world is still in bondage; and Satan and evil hold sway.

Ask of Me. The Father holds Himself in the attitude of Giver, and a petition to God the Father empowers all agencies, inspires all movements. The Gospel is divinely inspired, and behind all its inspirations is prayer. Standing as the endowment of the enthroned Christ is the oath-bound covenant of the Father:

> *Ask of me, and I shall give thee the heathen for thine inheritance, and the uttermost parts of the earth for thy possession.*　　　　*(Ps. 2:8)*

And men shall pray to Him continually. (See Psalm 72:15.)

The prayers of holy men are ever streaming up to God, as fragrant as the richest incense. And God, in many ways, is speaking to us, declaring His wealth and our impoverishment: "I am the Maker of all things; the wealth and glory are Mine. *Command ye Me."* (See Isaiah 45:11–12.) Nevertheless, we can have all that God has for us. *Command ye Me.* We can do all things by God's aid, and we can have the whole of His aid by asking. This is no figment of the imagination, no idle dream, no vain fancy.

The Gospel, in its success and power, depends on our ability to pray. The dispensations of God depend on man's ability to pray. And yet, conscious as we are of the importance of prayer, of its vital importance, we let the hours pass away as a blank. Fénelon,[1] a French prelate and writer of the late 1600s and early 1700s, has said:

> Of all the duties enjoined by Christianity, none is more essential and yet more neglected than prayer. Most people consider the exercise a fatiguing ceremony, which they are justified in abridging as much as possible. Even those whose profession or fears lead them to pray, pray with such languor and wanderings of mind that their prayers, far from drawing down blessings, only increase their condemnation.

---

[1] Fénelon (1651–1715): the shortened name of François de Salignac de La Mothe.

This is the way in which many, if not all, of us act about prayer; yet, in the end, we will only lament in death the irreparable loss that we have laid upon ourselves. The true Christian does not pray to stir himself up, but his prayer is the stirring up of himself to take hold of God.

When we calmly reflect upon the fact that the progress of our Lord's kingdom is dependent upon prayer, it is sad to think that we give so little time to the holy exercise. Everything depends on prayer, and yet we neglect it—not only to our own spiritual hurt, but also to the delay and injury of our Lord's cause upon earth. The forces of good and evil are contending for the world. If we would pray, we could add to the conquering power of the army of righteousness; and yet our lips are sealed, our hands hang listlessly by our sides, and by holding back from the prayer chamber we jeopardize the very cause in which we profess to be deeply interested.

Prayer is the one prime, eternal condition by which the Father is pledged to put the Son in possession of the world. Christ prays through His people. If there had been importunate, universal, and continuous prayer by God's people, the earth would have been possessed for Christ long before this. The delay is not to be accounted for by the inveterate obstacles, but by the lack of the right asking.

God has no force and demands no conditions but prayer. John Foster made this statement about the need for prayer in our lives:

> I am convinced that every man who, amidst his serious projects, is apprised of his dependence on God as completely as that dependence is a fact, will be impelled to pray and anxious to induce his serious friends to pray almost every hour. He will not without it promise himself any noble success any more than a mariner would expect to reach a distant coast by having his sails spread in a stagnation of air....The individual who should determine to try the last possible efficacy of prayer might probably find himself becoming a much more prevailing agent in his little sphere.

And, continued Foster, if more or all of the disciples of Christianity were to pray, with an earnest and unalterable resolution, in order that heaven should not withhold anything that the most persistent prayer could obtain, "it would be a sign that a revolution of the world was at hand."

Edward Payson[2] said of Foster's statement: "Probably very few missionaries, since the apostles, have tried the experiment. He who shall make the first trial will, I believe, effect wonders." Payson went on to say:

> Religion consists very much in giving God the place in our views and feelings that He actually fills in the universe. We know that in the universe He is all in all. Therefore, so far as He is constantly all in all to us, so far as we comply with the psalmist's charge to his soul, "My soul, wait thou only upon God" (Ps. 62:5), so far, I understand, have we advanced toward perfection.
>
> It is comparatively easy to wait upon God; but to wait upon Him only— to feel, so far as our strength, happiness, and usefulness are concerned, as if all creatures and second causes were annihilated, and we were alone in the universe with God—is, I suspect, a difficult and rare attainment. At least, I am sure it is one that I am very far from having made. In proportion as we make this attainment, we will find everything

---

[2] Edward Payson (1783–1827?): a Congregational preacher of New England.

easy; for we will become, emphatically, men of prayer; and we may say of prayer as Solomon says of money, that it "answereth all things" (Eccl. 10:19).

Again, John Foster, when approaching death, said:

> I never prayed more earnestly nor probably with such faithful frequency. "Pray without ceasing" has been the sentence repeating itself in my thoughts, and I am sure it must be my practice until the last conscious hour of life. Oh, why has it not been so throughout that long, indolent, inanimate half-century past?

We do more of everything else than of praying. As poor as our giving is, our contributions of money exceed our offerings of prayer. Perhaps, in the average congregation, fifty people aid in paying, while one saintly, ardent soul shuts himself up with God and wrestles for the deliverance of the heathen world. Official praying on set or state occasions counts for nothing in this estimate. We emphasize other things more than we do the necessity of prayer.

We often say prayers according to a certain prescription, but we do not have the world in the grasp of our faith. We are not praying in a way that moves God and brings all divine influences to help us. The world needs more true praying to save it from the reign and ruin of Satan.

We do not pray as Elijah prayed. John Foster put the whole matter very practically: "When the church of God is aroused to its obligation and duties and right faith to claim what Christ has promised—'all things whatsoever' (Matt. 21:22)—a revolution will take place."

But not all praying is true praying. The driving power, the conquering force in God's cause, must be God Himself. "Call unto me, and I will answer thee, and show thee great and mighty things, which thou knowest not" (Jer. 33:3), is God's challenge to pray. Prayer puts God in full force into His own work. "Ask me of things to come concerning my sons, and concerning the work of my hands command ye me" (Isa. 45:11), is God's carte blanche to prayer. Faith is only omnipotent when on its knees; and when its outstretched hands take hold of God, then it draws upon the utmost of God's capacity, for only a praying faith can get God's "all things whatsoever."

A marvelous prayer of the Old Testament—a prayer that I have already cited in an earlier chapter—is related again in the New

Testament in order to provoke and stimulate our praying. This prayer of Elijah is preceded with a declaration, the dynamic energy of which we can scarcely translate:

> *The effectual fervent prayer of a right-eous man availeth much. Elias was a man subject to like passions as we are, and he prayed earnestly that it might not rain: and it rained not on the earth by the space of three years and six months. And he prayed again, and the heaven gave rain, and the earth brought forth her fruit.* (James 5:16–18)

But why do we not obtain results by our praying? Why are our prayers not answered? Our lack of results, and the cause of all our feebleness in faith, was explained by the apostle James in these words:

> *Ye have not, because ye ask not. Ye ask, and receive not, because ye ask amiss, that ye may consume it upon your lusts.*
> *(James 4:2–3)*

Oneness with Christ is the glorious climax of spiritual attainment, because we can then "ask what [we] will, and it shall be done unto [us]" (John 15:7). Therefore, we must be one with Him. We must pray in His name, for prayer in Jesus' name puts the crowning crown on God; it glorifies Him through the Son and pledges the Son to give to men "whatsoever" and anything they ask. That is the whole truth, in a nutshell.

Chapter 4

Living in an Attitude of Prayer

In God's name, I beseech you, let prayer nourish your soul as your meals nourish your body. Let your fixed seasons of prayer keep you in God's presence through the day, and may His presence frequently remembered through it be an ever fresh spring of prayer. Such a brief, loving recollection of God renews a man's whole being, quiets his passions, supplies light and counsel in difficulty, gradually subdues the temper, and causes him to possess his soul in patience, or rather gives it up to the possession of God. —*Fénelon*

I t was said of the late Charles Spurgeon that he glided from laughter to prayer with the naturalness of one who lived in both elements. With him, the habit of prayer was free and unfettered. His life was not divided into compartments, the one shut off from the other with a rigid exclusiveness that barred all inter-communication. He lived in constant fellowship with his Father in heaven. He was ever in touch with God, and thus it was as natural for him to pray as it was for him to breathe.

"What a fine time we have had; let us thank God for it," he said to a friend on one occasion, when, out under the blue sky and wrapped in glorious sunshine, they had enjoyed a holiday with the unfettered enthusiasm of schoolboys. Prayer sprang as spontaneously to his lips as ordinary speech did, and there was never the slightest incongruity in his approach to the divine throne after any of his activities.

That is the attitude with regard to prayer that ought to mark every child of God. There are, and there ought to be, set seasons of communion with God, when everything else is shut out and we come into His presence to talk to Him and to let Him speak to us. And out of such seasons will spring that beautiful habit of prayer that weaves a golden bond between earth and heaven. Without these seasons of prayer, set as a pattern in our lives, the habit of prayer can never be formed; without them, there is no nourishment for the spiritual life. By means of them, the soul is lifted into a new atmosphere— the atmosphere of the heavenly city, in which it is easy to open the heart to God and to speak with Him as friend speaks with friend.

Thus, in every circumstance of life, prayer is the most natural outpouring of the soul, the unhindered turning to God for communion and direction. Whether in sorrow or in joy, in defeat or in victory, in weakness or in health, in calamity or in success, the heart leaps to meet with God, just as a child runs to his mother's arms, ever sure that her sympathy will meet every need.

Dr. Adam Clarke,[1] in his autobiography, recorded that, when Mr. Wesley[2] was returning to England by ship, considerable delay was caused by contrary winds. Wesley was reading, when he became aware of some confusion on board; and asking what was the matter, he was informed that the wind was contrary. "Then," was his reply, "let us go to prayer."

After Dr. Clarke had prayed, Wesley broke out into fervent supplication that seemed to be more the offering of faith than of mere desire. "Almighty and everlasting God," he prayed, "You have sway everywhere, and all things serve the purpose of Your will. You hold the

---

[1] Adam Clarke (1760–1832): commentator and preacher within the early Methodist church.

[2] Wesley: John Wesley (1703–1791), an English theologian, evangelist, and the founder of Methodism.

winds in Your fists and sit upon the floods of water, and You reign as King forever. Command these winds and these waves, that they may obey You, and take us speedily and safely to the haven where we wish to go."

The power of this petition was felt by all. Wesley rose from his knees, made no remark, but took up his book and continued reading. Dr. Clarke went on deck, and to his surprise found the vessel under sail, standing on her right course. Nor did she change until she was safely at anchor. On the sudden and favorable change of wind, Wesley made no remark; he so fully expected to be heard that he took it for granted that he was heard.

That was prayer with a purpose—the definite and direct utterance of one who knew that he had the ear of God, and that God had the willingness as well as the power to grant the petition that he asked of Him.

Major D. W. Whittle, in an introduction to writings on the wonders of prayer, told this story about George Müller:[3]

> I met Mr. Müller in the express, the morning of our sailing from Quebec to Liverpool. About half an hour before the

---

[3] George Müller (1805–1898): German-born preacher, and founder of children's orphanages in England.

tender[4] was to take the passengers to the ship, he asked of the agent if a deck chair had arrived for him from New York. He was answered, "No," and told that it could not possibly come in time for the steamer. I had with me a chair I had just purchased, and told Mr. Müller of the place nearby, and suggested, as but a few moments remained, that he had better buy one at once.

His reply was, "No, my brother. Our heavenly Father will send the chair from New York. It is one used by Mrs. Müller. I wrote ten days ago to a brother, who promised to see it forwarded here last week. He has not been prompt, as I would have desired, but I am sure our heavenly Father will send the chair. Mrs. Müller is very sick on the sea, and has particularly desired to have this chair; and not finding it here yesterday, we have made a special prayer that our heavenly Father would provide it for us, and we will trust Him to do so."

As this dear man of God went peacefully on board, running the risk of Mrs. Müller making the trip without a

---

[4] Tender: a ship that attends other ships, or a boat that communicates between shore and a larger ship.

chair, when, for a couple of dollars, she could have been provided for, I confess I feared Mr. Müller was carrying his faith principles too far and not acting wisely. I was kept at the express office ten minutes after Mr. Müller left. Just as I started to hurry to the wharf, a team of horses drove up the street, and on top of a load just arrived from New York was Mr. Müller's chair.

It was sent at once to the tender and placed in my hands to take to Mr. Müller, just as the boat was leaving the dock (the Lord having a lesson for me). Mr. Müller took it with the happy, pleased expression of a child who has just received a kindness deeply appreciated, and reverently removing his hat and folding his hands over it, he thanked the heavenly Father for sending the chair.

One of Melancthon's[5] correspondents wrote of Luther's praying:

I cannot enough admire the extraordinary cheerfulness, constancy, faith, and hope of the man in these trying and

---

[5] Melancthon (1497–1560): German scholar and religious reformer.

vexatious times. He constantly feeds
these gracious affections by a very dili-
gent study of the Word of God. Not a day
passes in which he does not employ in
prayer at least three of his very best
hours. Once I happened to hear him at
prayer. Gracious God! What spirit and
what faith is there in his expressions! He
petitions God with as much reverence as
if he were in the divine presence, and yet
with as firm a hope and confidence as he
would address a father or a friend.

"I know," he would say in his prayers, "You are our Father and our God;
and, therefore, I am sure You will bring
to naught the persecutors of Your children. For if You fail to do this, Your own
cause, being connected with ours, would
be endangered. It is entirely Your own
concern. We, by Your providence, have
been compelled to take a part. You,
therefore, will be our defense."

While I was listening to Luther
praying in this manner, at a distance,
my soul seemed on fire within me, to
hear the man address God so like a
friend, yet with so much gravity and
reverence; and also to hear him, in the
course of his prayer, insisting on the
promises contained in the Psalms, as if

he were sure his petitions would be granted.

Of William Bramwell, a Methodist preacher from England, noted for his zeal and prayer, the following has been related by a sergeant major:

In July 1811, our regiment was ordered for Spain, then the seat of a prolonged and bloody war. My mind was painfully exercised with the thoughts of leaving my dear wife and four helpless children in a strange country, unprotected and unprovided for. Mr. Bramwell felt a lively interest in our situation, and his sympathizing spirit seemed to drink in all the agonized feelings of my tender wife. He supplicated the throne of grace day and night on our behalf.

My wife and I spent the evening previous to our march at a friend's house, in company with Mr. Bramwell, who sat in a very pensive mood and appeared to be in a spiritual struggle the entire time. After supper, he suddenly took his hand from his chest, laid it on my knee, and said: "Brother Riley, mark what I am about to say! You are not to go to Spain. Remember, I tell you, you are not; for I have been wrestling with God on your behalf, and when my heavenly Father condescends in mercy to bless me with power to lay hold on Himself, I do not easily let Him go; no, not until I am favored with an answer. Therefore, you may depend on it, that the next time I hear from you, you will be settled in quarters." This came to pass exactly as he said. The next day the order for going to Spain was countermanded.

These men prayed with a purpose. To them, God was not far away, in some inaccessible region, but near at hand, ever ready to listen to the call of His children. There was no barrier between. They were on terms of perfect intimacy, if one may use such a phrase in relation to man and his Maker. No cloud obscured the face of the Father from His trusting child, who could look up into the divine countenance and pour out the longings of his heart. And that is the type of prayer that God never fails to hear. He knows that it comes from a heart at one with His own, from one who is entirely yielded to the heavenly plan, and so He bends His ear and gives to the pleading child the assurance that his petition has been heard and answered.

Have we not all had some such experience when we have approached the face of our Father with set and undeviating purpose? In an agony of soul, we have sought refuge from the oppression of the world in the anteroom of heaven; the waves of despair seemed to threaten destruction, and as no way of escape was visible anywhere, we fell back, like the disciples of old, upon the power of our Lord, crying to Him to save us lest we perish. (See Luke 8:24.) And then, in the twinkling of an eye, the thing was done. The billows sank into a calm; the howling wind died down at the divine command; the agony of the soul passed into a restful peace as over the whole being there crept the consciousness of the divine presence, bringing with it the assurance of answered prayer and sweet deliverance.

"I tell the Lord my troubles and difficulties, and wait for Him to give me the answers to them," said one man of God.

And it is wonderful how a matter that looked very dark will in prayer become crystal clear by the help of God's Spirit. I think Christians fail so often to get answers to their prayers because they do not wait long enough on God. They just drop down and say a few words, and then jump up and forget it and expect God to answer them. Such praying always reminds me of the small boy ringing his neighbor's doorbell, and then running away as fast as he can go.

When we acquire the habit of prayer, we enter into a new atmosphere. "Do you expect to go to heaven?" asked someone of a devout Scotsman. "Why, sir, I live there," was the quaint and unexpected reply. It was an elegant yet compelling statement of great truth, for the entire way to heaven is already the beginning of heaven to the Christian who walks near enough to God to hear the secrets He has to impart.

This attitude is beautifully illustrated in a story of Horace Bushnell,[6] told by Dr. Parkes Cadman. Bushnell was found to be suffering from an incurable disease. One evening, the Rev. Joseph Twichell visited him, and, as they sat together under the starry sky, Bushnell said, "One of us ought to pray." Twichell asked Bushnell to do so, and Bushnell began his prayer. Burying his face in the earth, he poured out his heart until, said Twichell, in recalling the incident, "I was afraid to stretch

---

[6] Horace Bushnell (1802–1876): American theologian.

out my hand in the darkness lest I should touch God."

To have God thus near is to enter the Holy of Holies—to breathe the fragrance of the heavenly air, to walk in Eden's delightful gardens. Nothing but prayer can bring God and man into this happy communion. That was the experience of Samuel Rutherford,[7] just as it is the experience of everyone who passes through the same gateway. When this saint of God was at one time confined in jail because he refused to act against his convictions, he enjoyed, in a rare degree, the divine companionship, recording in his diary that Jesus entered his cell, and that at His coming "every stone flashed like a ruby."

Many others have borne witness to the same sweet fellowship, when prayer had become the one habit of life that meant more than anything else to them. David Livingstone[8] lived in the realm of prayer and knew its gracious influence. It was his habit every birthday to write a prayer; and on the next to the last

---

[7] Samuel Rutherford: Scottish author of *Lex, Rex or, the Law and the Prince* (1644), in which the divine right of kings was challenged. Rutherford was placed under house arrest for his assertion that the basic premise of government and law must be the Bible, and he was awaiting execution when he died.

[8] David Livingstone (1813–1873): Scottish missionary and explorer in Africa.

birthday of all, this was his prayer: "O Divine One, I have not loved You earnestly, deeply, sincerely enough. Grant, I pray You, that before this year is ended I may have finished my task." It was just on the threshold of the year that followed that his faithful men, as they looked into the hut of Ilala, while the rain dripped from the eaves, saw their master on his knees beside his bed in an attitude of prayer. He had died on his knees in prayer.

Stonewall Jackson was a man of prayer. He said: "I have so fixed the habit in my mind that I never raise a glass of water to my lips without asking God's blessing, never seal a letter without putting a word of prayer under the seal, never take a letter from the mailbox without a brief sending of my thoughts heavenward, never change my classes in the lecture room without a minute's petition for the cadets who go out and for those who come in."

James Gilmour, the pioneer missionary to Mongolia, was a man of prayer. He had a habit in his writing of never using a blotter. He made a rule that when he got to the bottom of any page he would wait until the ink dried and spend the time in prayer.

In this way, the whole beings of these men were saturated with the divine, and they became the reflectors of the heavenly fragrance and glory. Walking with God down the avenues of prayer, we acquire something of His likeness, and unconsciously we become witnesses to others of His beauty and His grace. Professor James, in his famous work, *Varieties of Religious Experience,* told of a man of forty-nine who said:

God is more real to me than any thought or thing or person. I feel His presence positively, and even more as I live in closer harmony with His laws, as they are written in my body and mind. I feel Him in the sunshine or rain; my feelings are most nearly described by saying that everything is mingled with a delicious restfulness. I talk to Him as to a companion in prayer and praise, and our communion is delightful. He answers me again and again, often in words so clearly spoken that it seems my outer ear must have carried the tone, but generally in strong mental impressions. Usually a text of Scripture will unfold to me some new view of Him and His love for me, and His care for my safety. The knowledge that He is mine and I am His never leaves me; it is an abiding joy. Without it, life would be a blank, a desert, a shoreless, trackless waste.

Equally notable is the testimony of Sir Thomas Browne, the beloved physician who lived in Norwich, England, in 1605, and was the author of a very remarkable book of wide circulation, *Religio Medici*. In spite of the fact that England was passing through a period of national convulsion and political excitement, he found comfort and strength in prayer. "I have resolved," he wrote in a journal found among his private papers after his death, "to pray more and pray always, to pray in all places where quietness invites me to pray: in the house, on the highway, and on the street. And I have resolved to know no street or passage in this city that may not witness that I have not forgotten God." And he added:

> I purpose to take occasion of praying upon the sight of any church that I may pass, that God may be worshipped there in spirit, and that souls may be saved there. I purpose to pray daily for my sick patients and for the patients of other physicians; to say at my entrance into any home, "May the peace of God abide here"; to pray, after hearing a sermon, for a blessing on God's truth and upon the messenger; to bless God, upon the sight of a beautiful person, for

His creatures, and to pray for the beauty of such a soul, that God may enrich her with inward graces, and that the outward and inward may correspond; to pray God, upon the sight of a deformed person, to give them wholeness of soul, and by and by to give them the beauty of the resurrection.

What an illustration of the praying spirit! Such an attitude represents prayer without ceasing; it reveals the habit of prayer in its unceasing supplication, in its uninterrupted communion, in its constant intercession. What an illustration, too, of purpose in prayer! Of how many of us can it be said that as we pass people in the street we pray for them, or that as we enter a home or a church we remember the residents or the congregation in prayer to God?

The explanation of our thoughtlessness or forgetfulness lies in the fact that prayer, with so many of us, is simply a form of selfishness; it means asking for something for ourselves— that and nothing more.

And from such an attitude we need to pray to be delivered.

Chapter 5

The Energy of Prayer

The potency of prayer has subdued the strength of fire; it has bridled the rage of lions, hushed anarchy to rest, extinguished wars, appeased the elements, expelled demons, burst the chains of death, expanded the gates of heaven, assuaged diseases, repelled frauds, rescued cities from destruction, stayed the sun in its course, and arrested the progress of the thunderbolt. Prayer is an all-efficient panoply, a treasure undiminished, a mine that is never exhausted, a sky unobscured by clouds, a heaven unruffled by the storm. It is the root, the fountain, the mother of a thousand blessings.

—St. Chrysostom

Are we praying as Christ did? Do we abide in Him? Are our pleas and spirit the overflow of His pleas and Spirit? Does love rule the spirit—perfect love?

These questions must be considered as proper and highly appropriate at a time like the present. We have every reason to fear that we are doing more of other things than prayer. This is not a praying age; it is an age of great activity, of great movements, but one in which the tendency is very strong to stress the seen and the material, and to neglect and discount the unseen and the spiritual. Prayer is the greatest of all forces because it honors God and brings Him into active aid.

There can be no substitute, no rival for prayer; it stands alone as the great spiritual force, and this force must be imminent and acting. It cannot be dispensed with during one generation, nor can it be held in abeyance if any great movement is to be advanced. Rather, it must be continuous and particular, always, everywhere, and in everything. The book of Revelation says nothing about prayer as a great duty or a hallowed service, but much about prayer in its aggregated force and energies. It is the prayer force, ever living and ever praying; it is all saints' prayers going out as a mighty, living energy, while the lips that uttered the words may be stilled and sealed in death. The living church has an energy of faith to inherit the forces of all the past praying and to make it deathless.

But we cannot run our spiritual operations on the prayers of the past generations. Many people believe in the efficacy of prayer, but not many people pray. Prayer is the easiest and hardest of all things. It is the simplest and the most sublime, the weakest and the most powerful. Its results lie outside the range of human possibilities; they are limited only by the omnipotence of God.

Few Christians have anything but a vague idea of the power of prayer; fewer still have any experience of that power. The church seems almost wholly unaware of the power God puts into her hand. This spiritual carte blanche on the infinite resources of God's wisdom and power is rarely, if ever, used—never used to the full measure of honoring God. It is astounding how little we use it, and how little we reap its benefits. Prayer is our most formidable weapon, but the one in which we are the least skilled and the most averse to using. We do everything else for the heathen, except the thing God wants us to do. Prayer is the only thing that does any good, the only thing that makes effective everything else that we do.

Yet, in spite of the benefits and blessings that flow from communion with God, the sad confession must be made that we are not praying much. A comparatively very small number lead in prayer at the meetings. Fewer still pray with their families. Fewer still are in the habit of praying regularly in their prayer closets. Meetings specially for prayer are as rare as frost in June. In many churches there is neither the name nor the semblance of a prayer meeting. In the town and city churches, the prayer meeting in name is not a prayer meeting in fact. A sermon or a lecture is the main feature. Prayer is only the nominal attachment.

Our people are not essentially a praying people. That is evident by their lives.

Prayer is a trade to be learned, and it is a life trade. We must be apprentices and serve our time at it. Painstaking care, much thought, practice, and labor are required to be a skillful tradesman in praying. Practice in this, as well as in all other trades, makes perfect. One who is clumsy in the trade of praying will also mishandle the trade of salvation. Only toiling hands and hearts will make the workers proficient in this heavenly trade.

Prayer and a holy life are one. They mutually act and react. Neither can survive alone, for the absence of the one is the absence of the other. The hindrances of prayer are the hindrances in a holy life; and the conditions of praying are the conditions of righteousness, holiness, and salvation. The piety of saints is made, refined, and perfected by prayer. The first and last stages of holy living are crowned with praying.

A bird's-eye view of what has been accomplished by prayer shows what we lost when the dispensation of real prayer was substituted with pharisaical pretense and sham. It shows, too, how imperative is the need for holy men and women who will give themselves to earnest, Christlike praying. Monks, in general, have spoken ill of prayer; and they have substituted superstition for praying, and hypocritical ceremonies and routines for a holy life. And so, those who have been thought to live holy and pious lives, have turned out to be poor examples to the rest of believers.

We are all in danger of substituting church work and a ceaseless round of showy activities for prayer and holy living. A holy life does not live in the closet, but it cannot live without the prayer closet. If, by any chance, a person should establish a prayer chamber but not have an accompanying holy life, it would be a chamber without the presence of God in it.

The burden of the apostolic effort and the keynote of apostolic success is this: Put the saints everywhere to the task of praying. The

Gospel moves with slow and timid pace when the saints are not at their prayers early and late and long. Jesus Christ strove to put the saints to this task in the days of His personal ministry. He was moved with infinite compassion at seeing the ripened fields of earth perishing for lack of laborers (see Matthew 9:37–38); and, pausing in His own praying, He tried to awaken the sleeping sensibilities of His disciples to the duty of prayer, as He charged them: "Pray ye therefore the Lord of the harvest, that he will send forth labourers into his harvest" (v. 38). "And he spake a parable unto them to this end, that men ought always to pray" (Luke 18:1).

Before Pentecost, the apostles could get only glimpses of this great importance of prayer. But, when the Spirit came and filled them on Pentecost, prayer was elevated to its vital and all-commanding position in the Gospel of Christ. Now the call of prayer to every saint is the Spirit's loudest and most urgent call.

Where are the Christlike leaders who can teach the modern saints how to pray? Where are the leaders who will put them to the task? Do our leaders know we are raising up a prayerless set of saints? Where are the apostolic leaders who can put God's people to praying? Let them come to the front and do the work, and it will be the greatest work that can be done.

An increase of educational facilities and a great increase of financial support will be the most disastrous curse to religion, if these things are not sanctified by more and better praying than we are doing. And more praying will not just happen. We are a generation of non-praying saints who, like beggars, have neither the ardor nor the beauty nor the power of saints. Who will restore this branch? (See John 15:2–5.) We greatly need someone who can set the saints to this business of praying; and the one who can set the church to praying will be the greatest of reformers and apostles.

The campaign for the twentieth or thirtieth century will not help our praying, but it will hinder it if we are not careful. Nothing but a specific effort from a praying leadership will avail. None but praying leaders can have praying followers. Praying apostles will beget praying saints. A praying pulpit will beget praying pews.

Holy men have, in the past, changed the whole force of affairs; they have revolutionized character and country by prayer. And such achievements are still possible for us. The power is only waiting to be used. Prayer is simply the expression of faith.

I do not have enough time to tell of the mighty things effected by prayer, for by it holy ones have

> *subdued kingdoms, wrought righteous-*
> *ness, obtained promises, stopped the*
> *mouths of lions, quenched the violence of*
> *fire, escaped the edge of the sword, out of*
> *weakness were made strong, waxed val-*
> *iant in fight, turned to flight the armies*
> *of the aliens.* (Heb. 11:33–34)

Prayer honors God; it dishonors self. It is man's plea of weakness, ignorance, need—a plea that heaven cannot disregard. God delights to have us pray.

Prayer is not the opposite of work; it does not paralyze activity. Rather, prayer itself is the greatest work; it works mightily. It springs activity, stimulates desire and effort. Prayer is not an opiate, but a tonic; it does not lull to sleep, but arouses anew for action. The lazy man does not, cannot pray, for prayer demands energy. Paul calls it a striving, an agony. (See Romans 15:30.) With Jacob it was a wrestling; with the Syrophenician woman it was a struggle that called into play all the higher qualities of the soul, and that demanded great force to meet it.

The prayer closet is not an asylum for the indolent and worthless Christian. It is not a nursery where none but babes belong. It is the battlefield of the church, its citadel, the scene of heroic and unearthly conflicts. The closet is the base of supplies for the Christian and the church. Cut off from it, there is nothing left but retreat and disaster. The energy for work, the mastery over self, the deliverance from fear, and all spiritual results and graces, are much advanced by prayer.

The differences in the strength, experience, and holiness of one Christian compared with another, are found in the contrast in their praying. A man whose prayers are few, short, and feeble is surely a man of low spiritual condition; whereas the eminent Christian is the man who has been eminent in prayer. Men ought to pray much and ought to apply themselves to prayer. The deep things of God are learned only in prayer. Great things for God are done by great prayers. He who prays much, studies much, loves much, and works much, does much for God and humanity. The execution of the Gospel, the vigor of faith, the maturity and excellence of spiritual graces wait on prayer. Therefore, we ought to pray often, with both energy and perseverance.

Chapter 6

Persistence in Prayer

"Nothing is impossible to industry," said one of the seven sages of Greece. *Let us change the word "industry" to "persevering prayer," and the motto will be more Christian and more worthy of universal adoption. I am persuaded that we are all more deficient in a spirit of prayer than in any other grace. God loves importunate prayer so much that He will not give us much blessing without it. And the reason that He loves such prayer is that He loves us and knows that it is a necessary preparation for our receiving the richest blessings that He is waiting and longing to bestow.* —Adoniram Judson

Throughout His ministry, Christ made it clear that importunity is a distinguishing characteristic of true praying. We must not only pray, but we must also pray with great urgency, with intensity, and with repetition. We must not only pray, but we must also pray again and again. We must not get tired of praying. We must be thoroughly in earnest, deeply concerned about the things for which we ask, for Jesus Christ made it very plain that the secret of prayer and its success lie in its urgency. We must press our prayers upon God.

Adoniram Judson[1] said, "I never prayed sincerely and earnestly for anything but it came at some time. No matter at how distant a day, somehow, in some shape, probably the last I would have devised, it came." Oh, that we could all know this and know it well!

In a parable of exquisite pathos and simplicity, our Lord taught not simply that men ought to pray, but that men ought to pray with full heartiness, and press the matter with vigorous energy and courage.

> *And he spake a parable unto them to this end, that men ought always to pray, and not to faint; saying, There was in a city a judge, which feared not God, neither regarded man: and there was a widow in that city; and she came unto him, saying, Avenge me of mine adversary. And*

---

[1] Adoniram Judson (1788–1850): American Baptist missionary.

he would not for a while: but afterward
he said within himself, Though I fear
not God, nor regard man; yet because
this widow troubleth me, I will avenge
her, lest by her continual coming she
weary me. And the Lord said, Hear what
the unjust judge saith. And shall not
God avenge his own elect, which cry day
and night unto him, though he bear long
with them? I tell you that he will avenge
them speedily. Nevertheless when the
Son of man cometh, shall he find faith
on the earth? (Luke 18:1–8)

This poor woman's case was a most hope-
less one, but importunity brought hope from
the realms of despair and created success
where neither success nor its conditions existed. There is no stronger case to show how
our unwearied and dauntless prayer gains its
ends where everything else fails. The preface
to this parable says: "He spake a parable unto
them to this end, that men ought always to
pray, and not to faint" (v. 1). He knew that
men would soon grow fainthearted in praying;
so, to encourage us, He gives this picture of the
marvelous power of persistence in prayer.

The widow, weak and helpless, is helpless-
ness personified; bereft of every hope and influence that could move an unjust judge, she yet

wins her case solely by her tireless and offensive requests. Could the necessity of importunity, its power and tremendous importance in prayer, be pictured in deeper or more impressive coloring? Importunate prayer surmounts or removes all obstacles, overcomes every resisting force, and gains its ends in the face of invincible hindrances. We can do nothing without prayer, but all things can be done by importunate prayer. That is the teaching of Jesus Christ.

Another parable spoken by Jesus enforces the same great truth. A man at midnight goes to his friend for a loan of a few loaves of bread. (See Luke 11:5–10.) His pleas are strong, based on friendship and the embarrassing and exacting demands of necessity, but these all fail. He gets no bread at first, so he stays and presses, and he waits and gains. Sheer importunity succeeded where all other pleas and influences had failed.

The case of the Syrophenician woman is a parable in action. (See Mark 7:24–30.) She was stopped in her approaches to Christ by the information that He would not see anyone. She was denied His presence, and then in His presence was treated with seeming indifference, with the chill of silence and unconcern. Yet she pressed and approached, and the pressure and approach were repulsed by the stern and crushing statement that He was not sent to her kith[2] or kind, that she was reprobated from His mission and power.

She was humiliated by being called a dog; yet she accepted all, overcame all, and won all by her humble, dauntless, invincible importunity. The Son of God, pleased, surprised, overpowered by her unconquerable persistence, said to her: "O woman, great is thy faith: be it unto thee even as thou wilt" (Matt. 15:28). Jesus Christ surrendered Himself to the importunity of a great faith. "And shall not God avenge his own elect, which cry day and night unto him, though he bear long with them?" (Luke 18:7).

Jesus Christ presents the ability to importune as one of the elements of prayer, one of the main conditions of prayer. The prayer of the Syrophenician woman is an example of the matchless power of persistence in prayer, of a conflict more real and involving more vital energy, endurance, and all the higher elements than was ever illustrated in the conflicts of Isthmia or Olympia.[3]

---

[2] Kith: familiar friends, neighbors, or relatives.

[3] Isthmia: the Isthmus of Corinth, where, in ancient times, biennial pan-Hellenic games were held. Similar festivals of athletic contests were held in ancient Greece on the plain of Olympia; these have been revived and are now known as the international Olympic Games.

The first lessons of persistence are taught in the Sermon on the Mount: "Ask, and it shall be given you; seek, and ye shall find; knock, and it shall be opened unto you" (Matt. 7:7). These are steps of advance,

> *for every one that asketh, receiveth; and he that seeketh, findeth; and to him that knocketh it shall be opened.* *(Matt. 7:8)*

Without persistence, prayers may go unanswered. Importunity is made up of the ability to hold on, to continue, to wait with unrelaxed and unrelaxable grasp, restless desire, and restful patience. Importunate prayer is not an incidental occurrence, but the main thing; not a performance, but a passion; not an option, but a necessity.

Prayer, in its highest form and its grandest success, assumes the attitude of a wrestler with God. Prayer is the contest, trial, and victory of faith—a victory not secured from an enemy, but from Him who tries our faith that He may enlarge it. He tests our strength to make us stronger. Few things give such quickened and permanent vigor to the soul as a long, exhaustive season of importunate prayer. It provides an experience, an epoch, a new calendar for the spirit; it gives a new life, a soldierly training, to religion.

The Bible never wearies in its illustration of the fact that the highest spiritual good is secured as the return of the highest form of spiritual effort. John Wesley put it in these words: "Bear up the hands that hang down, by faith and prayer; support the tottering knees. (See Hebrews 12:12.) Have you any days of fasting and prayer? Storm the throne of grace and persevere therein, and mercy will come down." There is neither encouragement nor room in the religion of the Scriptures for feeble desires, listless efforts, lazy attitudes. All must be strenuous, urgent, ardent. Inflamed desires and impassioned, unwearied insistence are the things that delight heaven.

God would have His children unalterably in earnest and persistently bold in their efforts. Heaven is too busy to listen to half-hearted prayers or to respond to hasty, thoughtless calls to God.

Our whole being must be in our praying; like John Knox,[4] we must say and feel, "Give me Scotland, or may I die." Our experience and revelations of God are born of our costly sacrifice, our costly conflicts, our costly praying. The wrestling, the all-night praying of Jacob (see Genesis 32:24–28) began an era never to

---

[4] John Knox (1514–1572): Scottish religious reformer.

be forgotten by him; it brought God to the rescue, changed Esau's attitude and conduct, changed Jacob's character, saved and affected his life, and entered into the habits of a nation.

Our seasons of importunate prayer cut themselves, like the print of a diamond, into our hardest places, and mark our characters with ineffaceable traces. They are the salient periods of our lives, the memorial stones that endure and to which we turn. (See 1 Samuel 7:12.)

Importunity, it may be repeated, is a condition of prayer. We are to press the matter, not with vain repetitions, but with urgent repetitions. We repeat, not to count the times, but to gain the answer to our prayer. We cannot quit praying, because heart and soul are in our prayers. We pray "with all perseverance" (Eph. 6:18); we hang on to our prayers because we live by them. We press our pleas because we must have them or die.

I have already shown that Christ gave us two most expressive parables to emphasize the necessity of importunity in praying. Perhaps Abraham lost Sodom by failing to press, to the utmost, his privilege of praying. (See Genesis 18:16–33.) We know that Joash lost because he held off his smiting to appease an enemy king. (See 2 Kings 11:1–12:21.)

Perseverance counts much with God, just as it does with man. If Elijah had ceased at his first petition, the heavens would scarcely have yielded their rain to his feeble praying. (See James 5:17–18.) If Jacob had quit praying at decent bedtime, he would hardly have survived the next day's meeting with Esau. If the Syrophenician woman had allowed her faith to faint by silence, humiliation, or rejection, or to stop midway in its struggles, her grief-stricken home would never have been brightened by the healing of her daughter.

Pray and never faint, is the motto Christ gives us for praying. It is the test of our faith, and the more severe the trial and the longer the waiting, the more glorious the results.

The benefits and necessity of importunity are taught by the lives of the Old Testament saints. Praying men must be strong in hope and faith and prayer. They must know how to wait and to press, to wait on God and be in earnest in their approaches to Him.

Abraham left us an example of importunate intercession in his passionate pleading with God on behalf of Sodom and Gomorrah. If, as already indicated, he had not ceased in his asking, perhaps God would not have ceased in His giving. "Abraham left off asking before God left off granting," is how the saying goes.

Moses taught the power of importunity when he interceded for Israel forty days and forty nights, by fasting and prayer. And he succeeded in his importunity.

Jesus, in His teaching and example, illustrated and perfected this principle of Old Testament pleading and waiting. What a mystery that the only Son of God should be under the law of prayer—He who came on a mission direct from His Father, He whose only heaven on earth, whose only life and law, were to do His Father's will in that mission. How strange that the blessings that came to Him were impregnated and purchased by prayer. It is stranger still that importunity in prayer was the process by which His wealthiest supplies from God were gained.

Had He not prayed with importunity, no transfiguration would have been in His history, no mighty works would have rendered His career divine. His all-night praying was that which filled His all-day work with compassion and power. The importunate praying of His life crowned His death with triumph. He learned the high lesson of submission to God's will in the struggles of importunate prayer, before He illustrated that submission so sublimely on the cross.

Charles Spurgeon has said:

Whether we like it or not, asking is the rule of the kingdom. "Ask, and ye shall receive" (John 16:24). It is a rule that never will be altered in anybody's case. Our Lord Jesus Christ is the elder brother of the family, but God has not relaxed the rule even for Him. Remember this text: Jehovah says to His own Son, "Ask of me, and I shall give thee the heathen for thine inheritance, and the uttermost parts of the earth for thy possession" (Ps. 2:8). If the royal and divine Son of God cannot be exempted from the rule of asking that He may have, you and I cannot expect the rule to be relaxed in our favor. Why should it be?

What reason can be given why we should be exempted from prayer? What argument can there be why we should be deprived of the privilege and delivered from the necessity of supplication? I can see none; can you? God will bless Elijah and send rain on Israel, but Elijah must pray for it. If the chosen nation is to prosper, Samuel must plead for it. If the Jews are to be delivered, Daniel must intercede. God will bless Paul, and the nations will be converted through him, but Paul must pray. Indeed, he did pray without ceasing; his epistles show that he expected nothing except by asking for it. If you may have everything by asking, and nothing without asking, I beg you to see how absolutely vital prayer is, and I beseech you to abound in it.

I have no doubt that much of our praying fails for lack of persistence. So many of our prayers are said without the fire and strength of perseverance. Persistence is the essence of true praying. It may not be always called into exercise, but it must be there as the reserve force. Jesus taught that perseverance is the essential element of prayer. Therefore, men must be in earnest when they kneel at God's footstool.

Too often we get fainthearted and quit praying at the point where we ought to begin. We let go at the very point where we should most strongly hold on. Consequently, our prayers are weak because they are not impassioned by an unfailing and resistless will.

God loves the importunate pleader, and sends him answers that would never have been granted but for the persistence that refuses to let go until the petition craved for is granted.

Chapter 7

Secret Prayer

Be sure you look to your secret duty; keep that up whatever you do. The soul cannot prosper in the neglect of it. Apostasy generally begins at the closet door. Be much in secret fellowship with God. It is secret trading that enriches the Christian. Let prayer be the key of the morning and the bolt at night. The best way to fight against sin is to fight it on our knees.

—Philip Henry

M en ought *always* to pray, and not to faint" (Luke 18:1, italics added). These words are the words of our Lord, who not only always sought to impress upon His followers the urgency and the importance of prayer, but also set them an example that they, unfortunately, have been far too slow to copy.

The *always* speaks for itself. Prayer is not a meaningless function or duty to be crowded into the busy or weary activities of the day; and we are not obeying our Lord's command when we content ourselves with a few minutes on our knees in the morning rush or late at night, when the faculties, tired with the tasks of the day, call out for rest. God is always ready to hear our call, it is true; His ear is ever attentive to the cry of His child, but we can never get to know Him if we use the vehicle of prayer as we use the telephone—for a few words of hurried conversation. Intimacy requires development. We can never know Him by brief and fragmentary and thoughtless repetitions of intercessions that are requests for personal favors and nothing more.

That is not the way in which we can come into communication with heaven's King. "The goal of prayer is the ear of God," said Charles Spurgeon; and this is a goal that can only be reached by patient and continuous waiting upon Him, by pouring out our hearts to Him, and permitting Him to speak to us. Only by so doing can we expect to know Him; and as we come to know Him better, we will spend more time in His presence and find that presence a constant and ever increasing delight.

Always does not mean that we are to neglect the ordinary duties of life; what it means is that the soul that has come into intimate contact with God in the silence of the prayer chamber is never out of conscious touch with the Father; that the heart is always going out to Him in loving communion; and that the moment the mind is released from the task upon which it is engaged, it returns as naturally to God as the bird does to its nest. What a beautiful conception of prayer we get if we regard it in this light, if we view it as a constant fellowship, an unbroken audience with the King! Prayer then loses every vestige of dread that it may once have possessed; we regard it no longer as a duty that must be performed, but rather as a privilege that is to be enjoyed, a rare delight that is always revealing some new beauty.

Thus, when we open our eyes in the morning, our thoughts instantly turn heavenward. To many Christians, the morning hours are the most precious portion of the day, because they provide the opportunity for the hallowed fellowship that gives the keynote to the day's program. And what better introduction can there be to the never ceasing glory and wonder of a new day than to spend it alone with God? It is said that D. L. Moody, at a time when no other place was available, kept his morning watch in the coal shed, pouring out his heart to God, and finding in his precious Bible a true "feast of fat things" (Isa. 25:6).

George Müller also combined Bible study with prayer in the quiet morning hours. At one time, his practice was to give himself to prayer in the morning, after having dressed. Then his plan underwent a change. As he himself put it,

> I saw the most important thing I had to do was to give myself to the reading of the Word of God, and to meditation on it, that thus my heart might be comforted, encouraged, warned, reproved, instructed; and that, by means of the Word of God, while meditating on it, my heart might be brought into communion with the Lord. I began, therefore, to meditate on the New Testament early in the morning.
>
> The first thing I did, after having asked in a few words for the Lord's blessing upon His precious Word, was to begin to meditate on the Word of God, searching, as it were, into every verse to get blessing out of it. I did this not for the sake of the public ministry of the Word, nor for the sake of preaching on what I had meditated on, but for the sake of obtaining food for my own soul.

Almost invariably, I have found the result to be that, after a very few minutes, my soul has been led to confession, or to thanksgiving, or to intercession, or to supplication; so that, though I did not, as it were, give myself to prayer, but to meditation, yet it turned almost immediately more or less into prayer.

The study of the Word and prayer go together, and we find that when the one is truly practiced, the other is sure to be seen in close alliance.

But we do not pray *always*. That is the trouble with so many of us. We need to pray much more than we do and much longer than we do.

It has been said of the gifted and saintly Robert Murray McCheyne, "Whether viewed as a son, a brother, a friend, or a pastor, he was the most faultless and attractive exhibition of the true Christian they had ever seen embodied in a living form." He knew what it was to spend much time upon his knees, and he never wearied in urging upon others the joy and the value of holy intercession. "God's children should pray," he said. "They should cry day and night unto Him. God hears every one of your cries in the busy hours of the daytime and in the lonely watches of the night." In every way, by preaching, by exhortation when present, and by letters when absent, McCheyne emphasized the vital duty of prayer, importunate and unceasing prayer.

In his diary we find this: "In the morning I was engaged in preparing the head, then the heart. This has been frequently my error, and I have always felt the evil of it, especially in prayer. Reform it then, O Lord."

While on his trip to the Holy Land, McCheyne wrote: "For much of our safety I feel indebted to the prayers of my people. If the veil of the world's machinery were lifted off, how much we would find done in answer to the prayers of God's children!"

In an ordination sermon he said to the preacher:

> Give yourself to prayers and the ministry of the Word. (See Acts 6:3–4.) If you do not pray, God will probably lay you aside from your ministry, as He did me, to teach you to pray. Remember Luther's maxim: "To have prayed well is to have studied well." Get your texts, your thoughts, your words from God. Carry the names of the little flock upon your breast like the high priest. (See Exodus

28:1–2, 15–21, 29.) Wrestle for the un-
converted.

Luther spent his last three hours in
prayer; John Welch prayed seven or
eight hours a day. He used to keep a
blanket on his bed that he might wrap
himself in when he rose during the
night. Sometimes his wife found him
lying on the ground, weeping. When she
complained, he would say, "O woman, I
have the souls of three thousand to answer for, and I know not how it is with
many of them."

McCheyne exhorted and charged the people:

Pray for your pastor. Pray for his
body, that he may be kept strong and
spared many years. Pray for his soul,
that he may be kept humble and holy, a
burning and shining light. Pray for his
ministry, that it may be abundantly
blessed, that he may be anointed to
preach good tidings. Let there be no secret prayer without naming him before
your God, no family prayer without carrying your pastor in your hearts to God.

Even McCheyne's biographer said of him:
"Two things he seems never to have ceased

from—the cultivation of personal holiness and the most anxious efforts to win souls." These two things are the inseparable attendants to the ministry of prayer. Prayer fails when the desire and effort for personal holiness fail.

No person is a soulwinner who is not an expert in the ministry of prayer. "It is the duty of ministers," said McCheyne, "to begin the reformation of religion and manner with themselves, their families, etc., with confession of past sin, and with earnest prayer for direction, grace, and full purpose of heart." He began with himself, with the following resolution, under the heading of "Reformation in Secret Prayer":

> I ought not to omit any of the parts of prayer—confession, adoration, thanksgiving, petition, and intercession. Proceeding from low views of God and His law, slight views of my heart, and the sin of my past life, there is a fearful tendency to omit *confession*. This must be resisted. There is a constant tendency to omit *adoration* when I forget to whom I am speaking, when I rush heedlessly into the presence of Jehovah without thought of His awe-inspiring name and character. When I have little

eyesight for His glory, and little admiration of His wonders, my heart has a native tendency to omit giving *thanks*, and yet it is specially commanded. Often when the heart is dead to the salvation of others, I omit *intercession*, and yet it especially is the spirit of the great Advocate who has the name of Israel on His heart.

I ought to pray before seeing anyone. Often when I sleep long or meet with others early, and then have family prayer and breakfast and forenoon callers, it is eleven or twelve o'clock before I begin secret prayer. This is a wretched system; it is unscriptural. Christ rose before day and went into a solitary place. David said, "Early will I seek thee" (Ps. 63:1), and, "My voice shalt thou hear in the morning" (Ps. 5:3). Mary Magdalene came to the sepulchre while it was yet dark.

Family prayer loses much of the power and sweetness of prayer; and I can do no good to those who come to seek from me if I have forgotten my time alone with God in the early morning. The conscience feels guilty, the soul unfed, the lamp not trimmed. (See Matthew 25:1-13.) I feel it is far better to begin with God, to see His face first, to get my soul near Him before it is near another. "When I awake, I am still with thee" (Ps. 139:18). If I have slept too long, or if I am going on an early journey, or if my time is in any way shortened, it is best to dress hurriedly and have a few minutes alone with God than to give up all for lost. But, in general, it is best to have at least one hour alone with God before engaging in anything else. I ought to spend the best hours of the day in communion with God. When I awake in the night, I ought to rise and pray as John Welch and David did.

McCheyne believed in being always in prayer; and his fruitful life, short though that life was, affords an illustration of the power that comes from long and frequent visits to the secret place where we keep tryst with our Lord.

Secret praying is the test, the gauge, the preserver of man's relation to God. The prayer chamber, while it is the test of the sincerity of our devotion to God, becomes also the measure of the devotion. The self-denial, the sacrifices that we make for our prayer chambers, the frequency of our visits to that hallowed place of meeting with the Lord, the lingering to stay, the loathsomeness to leave, are values that we put on communion alone with God; they are the price we pay for the Spirit's hours of heavenly love.

When the prayer chambers of saints are closed or are entered casually or coldly, then church rulers are secular, fleshly, materialistic; spiritual character sinks to a low level, and the ministry becomes restrained and enfeebled.

William Wilberforce,[1] high in social position, a member of Parliament, and the friend of the famous statesman William Pitt,[2] was not called by God to forsake his high social position or to quit Parliament, but he was called to order his life according to the pattern set by Jesus Christ and to give himself to prayer. To read the story of his life is to be impressed with his holiness and his devotion to the claims of the quiet hours alone with God. His conversion was announced to his friends—to Pitt and others—by letter.

In the beginning of his religious career he recorded:

---

[1] William Wilberforce (1759–1833): English philanthropist and abolitionist.

[2] William Pitt, Jr. (1759–1806): son of earlier English statesman, William Pitt, Sr. He was referred to as "The Younger Pitt."

My chief reasons for a day of secret prayer are that (1) the state of public affairs is very critical and calls for earnest deprecation of the divine displeasure; (2) my station in life is a very difficult one, wherein I am at a loss to know how to act; direction, therefore, should be specially sought from time to time; and (3) I have been graciously supported in difficult situations of a public nature. I have gone out and returned home in safety, and a kind reception has attended me. I would humbly hope, too, that what I am now doing is a proof that God has not withdrawn His Holy Spirit from me. I am covered with mercies.

The recurrence of his birthday led Wilberforce again to review his situation and employment. He wrote:

I find that books alienate my heart from God as much as anything. I have been framing a plan of study for myself; but let me remember but one thing is needful, that if my heart cannot be kept in a spiritual state without so much prayer, meditation, Scripture reading, etc., as are incompatible with study, I must *seek first* the righteousness of God.

Everything was to be surrendered for spiritual advance.

We also find him saying:

> I fear that I have not studied the Scriptures enough. Surely, in the summer recess, I ought to read the Scriptures an hour or two every day, besides prayer, devotional reading, and meditation. God will prosper me better if I wait on Him. The experience of all good men shows that, without constant prayer and watchfulness, the life of God in the soul stagnates.

Doddridge's[3] morning and evening devotions were serious matters. Colonel Gardiner always spent hours in prayer in the morning before he went forth. Bonnell practiced private devotions largely morning and evening, and repeated Psalms while both dressing and undressing, in order to raise his mind to heavenly things. I must look to God to make the means effectual. I fear that my devotions are too hurried, that I do not read the Scriptures enough. I must grow in grace; I must love God

---

[3] Doddridge: author of *Prize and Progress of Religion in the Soul.*

more; I must feel the power of divine things more. Whether I am more or less learned signifies nothing. Whether even I execute the work that I deem useful is comparatively unimportant. But beware, my soul, of lukewarmness.

The New Year began with Holy Communion and new vows. "I will press forward," wrote Wilberforce,

and labor to know God better and love Him more. Assuredly I may, because God will give His Holy Spirit to them that ask Him (see Luke 11:13), and the Holy Spirit will shed abroad the love of God in the heart. (See Romans 5:5.) Oh, then, pray, pray; be earnest, press forward (see Philippians 3:14) and follow on to know the Lord. (See Hosea 6:3.) Without watchfulness, humiliation, and prayer, the sense of divine things must languish.

To prepare for the future, he said he found nothing more effectual than private prayer and the serious perusal of the New Testament.

And again he wrote:

I must put down that I have lately too little time for private devotions. I can sadly confirm Doddridge's remark that when we go on ill in the prayer closet, we commonly do so everywhere else. I must mend here. I am afraid of getting into what Owen calls the trade of sinning and repenting. Lord, help me; the shortening of private devotions starves the soul; it grows lean and faint. This must not be. I must redeem more time. I see how lean in spirit I become without full allowance of time for private devotions; I must be careful to be watching unto prayer.

At another time Wilberforce put on record:

I must try what I long ago heard was the rule of E——— the great upholsterer, who, when he came from Bond Street to his little villa, always first retired to his closet. I have been keeping too late hours, and hence have had but a hurried half hour to myself. Surely the experience of all good men confirms the proposition, that without due measure of private devotions, the soul will grow lean.

To his son he wrote:

Let me implore you not to be seduced into neglecting, curtailing, or hurrying over your morning prayers. Of all things, guard against neglecting God in the prayer closet. There is nothing more fatal to the life and power of religion. More solitude and earlier hours—prayer three times a day, at least. How much better might I serve if I cultivated a closer communion with God!

Wilberforce knew the secret of a holy life. Is that not where most of us fail? We are so busy with other things, so immersed even in doing good and in carrying out the Lord's work, that we neglect the quiet seasons of prayer with God; and before we are aware of it, our souls are lean and impoverished.

The prayer chamber conserves our relation to God. It hems every raw edge; it tucks up every flowing and entangling garment (see 2 Timothy 2:4); it girds up every fainting loin. (See 1 Peter 1:13.) The sheet anchor[4] does not hold the ship more surely and safely than the prayer chamber holds us to God. Satan has to break our hold on, and close up our way to, the

---

[4] Sheet anchor: a large, strong anchor formerly carried in a ship and used as a spare in emergencies.

prayer chambers, before he can break our hold on God or close up our way to heaven.

"One night alone in prayer," said Spurgeon,

> might make us new men, changed from poverty of soul to spiritual wealth, from trembling to triumphing. We have an example of it in the life of Jacob. He was once the crafty shuffler, always bargaining and calculating, unlovely in almost every respect. Yet, one night in prayer turned the supplanter into a prevailing prince, and robed him with celestial grandeur. From that night, he lived on the sacred page as one of the nobility of heaven. Could we not, at least now and then, in these weary earthbound years, hedge about a single night for such enriching traffic with the skies?
>
> What, have we no sacred ambition? Are we deaf to the yearnings of divine love? Yet, my fellow believers, men will cheerfully quit their warm couches for wealth and for science. Can we not do it now and again for the love of God and the good of souls? Where is our zeal, our gratitude, our sincerity? I am ashamed while I thus upbraid both myself and

you. May we often tarry at Jabbok,[5] and cry with Jacob, as he grasped the angel—

> With thee all night I mean to stay,
> And wrestle till the break of day.

Surely, brethren, if we have given whole days to folly, we can afford a space for heavenly wisdom.

There was a time when we gave whole nights to chambering[6] and wantonness, to dancing and the world's revelry; we did not tire then; we were chiding the sun that he rose so soon, and wishing the hours would lag awhile that we might delight in wilder merriment and perhaps deeper sin. Oh, why then do we weary in heavenly employments? Why do we grow weary when asked to watch with our Lord? Up, sluggish heart, Jesus calls you! Rise and go forth to meet the heavenly Friend in the place where He manifests Himself.

We can never expect to grow in the likeness of our Lord unless we follow His example

---

[5] Jabbok: the river near which Jacob wrestled through the night with God; a tributary of the Jordan River.

[6] Chambering: lewd and immodest behavior.

and give more time to communion with the Father. A revival of real praying would produce a spiritual revolution.

> Be not afraid to pray; to pray is right;
>   Pray if thou canst with hope, but ever pray,
> Though hope be weak or sick with long delay;
>   Pray in the darkness if there be no light;
> And if for any wish thou dare not pray
>   Then pray to God to cast that wish away.

Chapter 8

Praying Men and Personal Purity

> *Let me burn out for God. After all, whatever God may appoint, prayer is the great thing. Oh, that I may be a man of prayer!*
> —Henry Martyn

Men of Wilberforce's character are needed today—praying men, who know how to give themselves to the greatest task demanding their time and their attention, men who can give their whole heart to the holy task of intercession, men who can pray through. God's cause is committed to men; indeed, God commits Himself to men. Praying men are the vicegerents[1] of God; they do His work and carry out His plans.

Yet men, in general, have quit praying. They are too busy to pray. Time and strength

---

[1] Vicegerent: an administrative deputy of a king or magistrate.

and every faculty are given over to money, to business, to the affairs of the world. Few men lay themselves out in great praying. The great business of praying is a hurried, petty, starved, beggarly business with most men.

Better praying and more of it—that is what we need. We need holier men, and more of them, holier women, and more of them to pray—women like Hannah, who, out of their greatest griefs and temptations brew their greatest prayers. (See 1 Samuel 1.) We are obliged to pray if we are citizens of God's kingdom. Prayerlessness is banishment, or worse, from God's kingdom. It is outlawry, a high crime, a constitutional breach. The Christian who relegates prayer to a subordinate place in his life soon loses whatever spiritual zeal he may once have possessed; and the church that makes little of prayer cannot maintain vital piety, and is powerless to advance the Gospel. The Gospel cannot live, fight, or conquer without prayer—prayer that is unceasing, instant, and ardent.

That the men in Paul's time had quit praying we cannot certainly affirm. Yet Paul called a halt, and laid a levy on men for prayer. "Put the men to praying" was Paul's unfailing remedy for great evils in the church, in the state, in business, and in the home. Put the men to praying, then politics will be cleansed, business will be thriftier, the church will be holier, the home will be sweeter.

> *I exhort therefore, that, first of all, sup-plications, prayers, intercessions, and giving of thanks, be made for all men; for kings, and for all that are in author-ity; that we may lead a quiet and peace-able life in all godliness and honesty. For this is good and acceptable in the sight of God our Saviour....I will* [or, desire] *therefore that men pray every where, lifting up holy hands, without wrath and doubting.* (1 Tim. 2:1–3, 8)

Praying women and children are invalu-able to God, but if their praying is not supple-mented by praying men, there will be a great loss in the power of prayer—a great breach and depreciation in the value of prayer, a great paralysis in the energy of the Gospel. As we have noted, Jesus Christ spoke a parable to the people, telling them that men ought always to pray and not faint (Luke 18:1). Men who are strong in everything else ought to be strong in prayer, and never yield to discouragement, weakness, or depression. Men who are brave, persistent, and respectable in other pursuits ought to be full of courage, unfainting, and strong-hearted in prayer.

Men are to pray; *all men* are to pray. Men, as distinguished from women, men in their strength, in their wisdom. Jesus presented an absolute, specific command that men should pray; it is an absolute, imperative necessity that men pray. The first of beings, man, should also be first in prayer.

The *men* are to pray for men. The direction in 1 Timothy is specific and classified. Just underneath it, however, we have a specific direction with regard to women. (See 1 Timothy 2:9–12.) The Bible here deals with the men in contrast to, and distinct from, the women, in relation to prayer, its importance, its wideness, and its practice. The men are definitely commanded, seriously charged, and strongly exhorted to pray. Perhaps it was that men were averse to prayer, or indifferent to it; it may be that they deemed it a small thing, and gave to it neither time nor value nor significance. But God would have all men pray, and so the great apostle lifted the subject into prominence and emphasized its importance.

Prayer is of transcendent importance, for it is the mightiest agent to advance God's work. The cause of God has no commercial age, no cultured age, no age of education, no age of money. But it has one golden age, and that is the age of prayer. Only praying hearts and hands can do God's work. When its leaders are men of prayer, when prayer is the prevailing element of worship, like incense that gives continual fragrance to its service, then the cause of God will be triumphant.

Prayer succeeds when all else fails. Prayer has won great victories and has rescued, with notable triumph, God's saints when every other hope was gone. Men who know how to pray are the greatest boon God can give to earth—they are the richest gift earth can offer heaven. Men who know how to use this weapon of prayer are God's best soldiers, His mightiest leaders.

Praying men are also God's chosen leaders. The distinction between the leaders that God brings to the front to lead and bless His people, and those leaders who owe their position of leadership to a worldly, selfish, unsanctified selection, is this: God's leaders are preeminently men of prayer. This distinguishes them as the simple, divine affirmation of their call, the seal of their separation by God. Whatever other graces or gifts they may have, the grace and gift of prayer towers above them all. In whatever else they may share or differ, in the gift of prayer they are one.

What would God's leaders be without prayer? Strip Moses of his power in prayer, a gift that made him eminent in the eyes of the heathen, and the crown is taken from his head, the food and fire of his faith are gone. Elijah, without his praying, would have neither record nor place in the divine legacy—his life would have been insipid and cowardly; its energy, defiance, and fire would have disappeared. Without Elijah's praying, the Jordan would never have yielded to the stroke of his mantle (see 2 Kings 2:6–8), nor would the stern angel of death have honored him with the chariot and horses of fire (vv. 9–11). The argument that God used to quiet the fears of Ananias and convince him of Paul's condition and sincerity (see Acts 9:10–15) is the epitome of Paul's history, the answer to his life and work: "Behold, he prayeth" (v. 11).

Paul, Luther, Wesley—what would these chosen ones of God be without the distinguishing and controlling element of prayer? They were leaders for God because they were mighty in prayer. They were not leaders because of brilliancy in thought, nor because of their exhaustless resources, their magnificent culture, or their natural endowment; but they were leaders because, by the power of prayer, they could command the power of God. *Praying men* means much more than "men who pray by habit." It means "men with whom prayer is a mighty force," an energy that moves heaven and pours untold treasures of good on earth.

Praying men are the men who have done so much for God in the past. They are the ones who have won the victories for God, and spoiled His foes. They are the ones who have set up His kingdom in the very camps of His enemies. It is no different today; there are no other conditions of success for our times. This century has no law that will suspend the necessity or force of prayer—no substitute by which its gracious ends can be secured.

Praying men keep the church safe from the materialism that is affecting all its plans and policies, and that is hardening its lifeblood. By this I mean that the secret and poisonous insinuation circulates, that the church is not so dependent on purely spiritual forces as it used to be—that changed times and changed conditions have brought it out of its spiritual straits and dependencies and put it where other forces can bear it to its climax.

A fatal snare of this kind has allured the church into worldly embraces, dazzled her leaders, weakened her foundations, and deprived her of much of her beauty and strength. Praying men are the saviors of the church from this material tendency. They pour into it the original spiritual forces, lift it off the sand-bars of materialism, and press it out into the ocean depths of spiritual power. Praying men keep God in the church in full force, keep His hand on the helm, and train the church in strength and trust.

The world is coming into the church at many points and in many ways. It oozes in; it pours in; it comes in with brazen front or soft, insinuating disguise; it comes in at the top and comes in at the bottom; and it percolates through many a hidden way. The only protection or rescue that we have from worldliness lies in our intense and radical spirituality; and our only hope for the existence and mainte-nance of this high, saving spirituality, under God, is in the purest and most aggressive lead-ership—a leadership that knows the secret power of prayer, the sign by which the church has conquered; and a leadership that has con-science, conviction, and courage to hold true to its symbols, true to its traditions, and true to the hidden resources of its power.

We need this prayerful leadership; we must have it, so that, by the perfection and beauty of its holiness, by the strength and ele-vation of its faith, by the potency and pressure of its prayers, by the authority and spotless-ness of its example, by the fire and contagion of its zeal, by the singularity, sublimity, and unworldliness of its piety, it may influence God, and hold and mold the church to its heavenly pattern.

How mightily such leaders are felt! How their flame arouses the church! How they stir it by the force of their Pentecostal presence! How they embattle and give victory by the conflicts and triumphs of their own faith! How they fashion it by the impress and importunity of their prayers! How they inoculate it by the contagion and fire of their holiness! How they lead the march in great spiritual revolutions! How the church is raised from the dead by the resurrection call of their sermons! Holiness emerges in their wake as flowers at the voice of spring; and where they tread, the desert blooms as the garden of the Lord. (See Isaiah 35:1.) God's cause demands such leaders along the whole line of official position, from subordinate to superior. How feeble, aimless, or worldly are our efforts; how demoralized and worthless for God's work are we without them!

These leaders are not given as a result of any power on the part of the church. They are God's gifts. Their being, their presence, their number, and their ability are the tokens of His favor; their lack the sure sign of His disfavor, the indication of His withdrawal. Let the church of God be on her knees before the Lord of Hosts, that He may more mightily endow the leaders we already have, and put others in rank, and lead all along the line of our embattled front.

We are left with this: only praying hands can build for God. They are God's mighty ones on earth, His master builders. They may be destitute of all else, but with the wrestlings and prevailings of a simple-hearted faith, they are mighty—the mightiest for God. Church leaders may be gifted in all else, but without this greatest of gifts, they are as Samson shorn of his locks, or as the temple without the divine presence or the divine glory and on whose altars the heavenly flame has died.

Praying men are needed in all fields of spiritual labor. There is no position in the church of God, high or low, that can be well filled without earnest prayer. There is no position where Christians are found that does not demand the full play of a faith that always prays and never faints. Praying men are needed in the house of business, as well as in the house of God, that they may order and direct trade, not according to the maxims of this world, but according to Bible precepts and the maxims of the heavenly life.

The number and efficiency of God's laborers in all lands is dependent on the men of prayer. By a divinely arranged process, the mightiness of these men of prayer increases the number and success of their consecrated labors. Prayer opens wide their doors of access, gives holy aptness to enter, and leads to holy boldness, firmness, and fruit.

Men of prayer are needed especially in the positions of church influence, honor, and power. These leaders of church thought, of church work, and of church life should be men of demonstrated power in prayer. It is the praying heart that sanctifies the toil and skill of the hands, and the toil and wisdom of the mind. Prayer keeps work in the line of God's will, and keeps thought in the line of God's Word. The solemn responsibilities of leadership in God's church, in a large or limited sphere, should be so hedged about with prayer that between it and the world there should be an impassable gulf; they should be so elevated and purified by prayer that neither cloud nor night can stain the radiance or dim the sight of a constant, meridian[2] view of God.

Many church leaders seem to think that if they can be prominent as men of business, of money or influence, of thought, of plans, of

---

[2] Meridian: elevated, pertaining to the highest point.

scholarly attainments, of eloquent gifts, of conspicuous activities, that these are enough, and
will atone for the absence of the higher spiritual power that only much praying can give.
But how vain and paltry are these achievements in the serious work of bringing glory to
God, controlling the church for Him, and
bringing it into full accord with its divine mission!

We are looking for praying men and holy
men—men of purity, whose presence in the
church will make it like a censer of holiest incense flaming up to God. With God, the man
counts for everything. Rites, forms, and organizations have little meaning; unless they
are backed by the holiness of the man, they are
offensive in God's sight.

> *Incense is an abomination unto me; the
> new moons and sabbaths, the calling of
> assemblies, I cannot away with; it is in-
> iquity, even the solemn meeting.*
>
> *(Isa. 1:13)*

Why has God spoken so strongly against
His own ordinances? Because personal purity
has failed. The impure man has tainted all the
sacred institutions of God and defiled them.
Men have built Him glorious temples and have

striven and exhausted themselves to please
God by all manner of gifts; but in lofty strains
He has rebuked these proud worshippers and
rejected their princely gifts:

> *Heaven is my throne, and the earth is*
> *my footstool: where is the house that ye*
> *build unto me? and where is the place of*
> *my rest? For all those things hath mine*
> *hand made, and all those things have*
> *been, saith the LORD....He that killeth*
> *an ox is as if he slew a man; he that sac-*
> *rificeth a lamb, as if he cut off a dog's*
> *neck; he that offereth an oblation, as if*
> *he offered swine's blood; he that burneth*
> *incense, as if he blessed an idol.*
> *(Isa. 66:1–3)*

Turning away in disgust from these costly and
profane offerings, He declares: "But to this
man will I look, even to him that is poor and of
a contrite spirit, and trembleth at my word" (v.
2).

This truth is fundamental, that God regards the personal purity of the man more
than He regards any sacrifice or any ceremony.
In fact, God has given so much regard to men
that He has put a kind of discount on all else.
This truth suffers when ordinances are made

much of and forms of worship multiply. The man and his spiritual character depreciate as church ceremonies increase. The simplicity of worship is lost in religious aesthetics, or in the gaudiness of religious forms.

This truth that the personal purity of the individual is the only thing for which God cares, is lost sight of when the church begins to value men for what they have. When the church in any way eyes a man's money, social standing, or belongings, then spiritual values are at a fearful discount; and the tears of penitence, the heaviness of guilt, are never seen at her portals. Worldly bribes have opened and stained the pearly gates of the church by the entrance of the impure.

This truth that God is looking for personal purity is swallowed up when the church has a greed for numbers. "Not numbers, but personal purity is our aim," said the fathers of Methodism. The parading of church statistics runs strongly against the grain of spiritual religion. Eyeing numbers greatly hinders the looking after personal purity. The increase of quantity is generally at a loss of quality. Bulk lessens preciousness.

The age of church organization and church machinery is not an age noted for elevated and strong personal piety. Machinery looks for engineers, and organizations look for managers or generals; but neither looks for saints to run its affairs. The simplest organization may aid purity as well as strength; but beyond that narrow limit, organizations swallow up the individual, and they are careless of personal purity. Activity, enthusiasm, and zeal for the organization of the church, come in as the vicious substitutes for spiritual character. Holiness and spiritual graces are discarded as too slow and too costly for the progress and rush of the age. Because of machinery, new organizations, and spiritual weakness, results are vainly expected to be secured that can only be secured by faith, prayer, and waiting on God.

The man and his spiritual character are what God is looking after. If men, holy men, can be turned out readier and better by the easy processes of church machinery than by the old-time processes, we would gladly invest in every new and improved patent; but we do not believe it. We adhere to the old way, the way the holy prophets went, the King's highway of holiness. (See Isaiah 35:8.)

So, once more, let us apply the emphasis and repeat that the great need of the church in this and all ages is for men of such commanding faith, of such unsullied holiness, of such marked spiritual vigor and consuming zeal, that they will work spiritual revolutions through their mighty praying. As someone has said,

Natural ability and educational advantages do not figure as factors in this matter; but a capacity for faith, the ability to pray, the power of a thorough consecration, the ability of self-littleness, an absolute losing of oneself in God's glory, and an ever present and insatiable yearning and seeking after all the fullness of God. Our need is for men who can set the church ablaze for God, not in a noisy, showy way, but with an intense and quiet heat that melts and moves everything for God.

Chapter 9

The Possibilities of Prayer

> *More things are wrought by prayer*
> *Than this world dreams of. Wherefore, let thy voice*
> *Rise like a fountain for me night and day.*
> *For what are men better than sheep or goats,*
> *That nourish a blind life within the brain,*
> *If, knowing God, they lift not hands of prayer*
> *Both for themselves and those who call them friend?*
> *For so the whole round earth is every way*
> *Bound by gold chains about the feet of God.*
> —Alfred, Lord Tennyson

It may be said with emphasis that no lazy saint prays. Can there be a lazy saint? Can there be a prayerless saint? Does not slack praying cut short sainthood's crown and kingdom? Can there be a cowardly soldier? Can there be a saintly hypocrite? Can there be virtuous vice? It is only when these impossibilities are brought into being that we then can find a prayerless saint.

To go through the motion of praying is a dull business, though not a difficult one. To say prayers in a decent, delicate way is not heavy work. But to really pray, to pray until hell feels the ponderous stroke, to pray until the iron gates of difficulty are opened, to pray until the mountains of obstacles are removed, or until the mists are exhaled and the clouds are lifted, and the sunshine of a cloudless day brightens—this is hard work, but it is God's work and man's best labor. Never was the toil of hand, head, and heart less spent in vain than when praying.

It may be difficult to wait and press and pray, and hear no voice, but you must stay until God answers. The joy of answered prayer is the joy of a travailing mother when a son is born into the world, the joy of a slave whose chains have been burst asunder and to whom new life and liberty have just come.

It is not an easy thing to pray. Behind the praying, all the conditions of prayer must be met. These conditions are possible, but they are not to be seized on in a moment by the prayerless. Of course, they may exist in the faithful and holy, but they cannot exist in or be met by a frivolous, negligent, laggard spirit.

Prayer does not stand alone. It is not an isolated performance. Prayer stands in closest connection with all the duties of an ardent piety. It comes as a result of a vigorous and commanding faith. Prayer honors God, acknowledges His being, exalts His power, adores His providence, secures His aid. But to pray well is to do all things well. A sneering half-rationalism cries out against devotion, that it does nothing but pray. If it is true that devotion does nothing but pray, then it does nothing at all. To do nothing but pray fails to do the praying, for the antecedent, coincident, and subsequent conditions of prayer are but the sum of all the energized forces of a practical, working piety.

Prayer, like faith, obtains promises, enlarges their operation, and adds to the measure of their results. The possibilities of prayer run parallel with the promises of God. Prayer opens an outlet for the promises, removes the hindrances in the way of their execution, puts them into working order, and secures their gracious ends. God's promises were to Abraham and to his seed, but a barren womb and many obstacles stood in the way of the fulfillment of these promises; nevertheless, prayer removed them all, made a highway for the promises, added to the facility and speediness of their realization; and by prayer the promise shone bright and perfect in its execution.

The possibilities of prayer are found in its alliance with the purposes of God, for God's purposes and man's praying are the combination of all potent and omnipotent forces. More than this, the possibilities of prayer are seen in the fact that prayer changes the purposes of God. It is in the very nature of prayer to plead and give directions. Prayer is not a negation; it is a positive force. It never rebels against the will of God, never comes into conflict with that will, but it is evident that it does seek to change God's purposes.

Christ said, "The cup which my Father hath given me, shall I not drink it?" (John 18:11), and yet He had prayed that very night, "If it be possible, let this cup pass from me" (Matt. 26:39). Paul sought to change the purposes of God about the thorn in his flesh. (See 2 Corinthians 12:7–9.) God was set on destroying Israel, and the prayer of Moses changed the purposes of God and saved the nation. (See Deuteronomy 9:12–21.) In the time of the judges, the people of Israel were apostate and greatly oppressed. They repented and cried unto God, and He said: "Ye have forsaken me, and served other gods: wherefore I will deliver you no more" (Judg. 10:13). But they humbled themselves and put away their strange gods, and God's "soul was grieved for the misery of Israel" (v. 16). In His mercy, He sent them deliverance by Jephthah.

God sent Isaiah to say to Hezekiah, "Set thine house in order; for thou shalt die, and not live" (2 Kings 20:1). So Hezekiah prayed, and God sent Isaiah back to say, "I have heard thy prayer, I have seen thy tears: behold...I will add unto thy days fifteen years" (vv. 5–6).

"Yet forty days, and Nineveh shall be overthrown" (Jonah 3:4) was God's message by Jonah. But Nineveh cried mightily to God, and "God repented of the evil, that he had said that he would do unto them; and he did it not" (v. 10).

The possibilities of prayer may be seen from the various conditions it reaches and the diverse ends it secures. Elijah prayed over a dead child, and he came to life; Elisha did the same thing. Christ prayed at Lazarus's grave, and Lazarus came forth. Peter kneeled down and prayed beside dead Dorcas, and she opened her eyes and sat up; and Peter presented her alive to the distressed company. Paul prayed for Publius' father and he was healed. Jacob's praying changed Esau's murderous hate into the kisses of the tenderest brotherly embrace.

God gave Jacob and Esau to Rebecca because Isaac prayed for her. Joseph was the child of Rachel's prayers. Hannah's praying gave Samuel to Israel. John the Baptist was given to Elizabeth, barren and past the age of childbearing, in answer to the prayer of Zacharias. Elisha's praying brought famine or harvest to Israel; as he prayed, so it was. Ezra's praying carried the Spirit of God in heartbreaking conviction to the entire city of Jerusalem, and brought them, in tears of repentance, back to God. Isaiah's praying carried the shadow of the sun back ten degrees on the dial of Ahaz.

In answer to Hezekiah's praying, an angel slew one hundred and eighty-five thousand of Sennacherib's army in one night. Daniel's praying opened to him the vision of prophecy, helped him to administer the affairs of a mighty kingdom, and sent an angel to shut the lions' mouths. The angel was sent to Cornelius, and the Gospel was opened through Cornelius to the Gentile world, because his "prayers and...alms [had become] a memorial before God" (Acts 10:4).

"And what shall I more say? for the time would fail me to tell of Gedeon, and of Barak, and of Samson, and of Jephthae; of David also, and Samuel, and of the prophets" (Heb. 11:32); of Paul and Peter, and John and the apostles, and the holy company of saints, reformers, and martyrs, who, through praying,

> *subdued kingdoms, wrought righteous-*
> *ness, obtained promises, stopped the*
> *mouths of lions, quenched the violence of*
> *fire, escaped the edge of the sword, out of*
> *weakness were made strong, waxed val-*
> *iant in fight, turned to flight the armies*
> *of the aliens.* (Heb. 11:33–34)

Prayer puts God in the matter with commanding force: "Ask me of things to come concerning my sons," says God, "and concerning
the work of my hands command ye me" (Isa.
45:11). We are charged in God's Word "always
to pray" (Luke 18:1), "in every thing by
prayer" (Phil. 4:6), "continuing instant in
prayer" (Rom. 12:12), to "pray every where" (1
Tim. 2:8), "praying always" (Eph. 6:18). And
the promise is as immeasurable as the command is comprehensive: "All things, whatsoever ye shall ask in prayer, believing, ye shall
receive" (Matt. 21:22); "whatsoever ye shall
ask in my name, that will I do" (John 14:13);
"if ye shall ask any thing" (v. 14); "ye shall ask
what ye will, and it shall be done unto you"
(John 15:7); "whatsoever ye shall ask the Father...he will give it you" (John 16:23).

If there is anything not involved in the
words *all things whatsoever,* or not found in
the phrase *ask anything,* then these things

may be left out of prayer. Language could not cover a wider range, nor involve more fully all of the smallest details. These statements are only samples of the all-comprehending possibilities of prayer under the promises of God to those who meet the conditions of right praying.

These passages, though, give only a general outline of the immense regions over which prayer extends its influence. Beyond these, the effects of prayer reach and secure good from regions that cannot be traversed by language or thought.

Paul exhausted both language and thought in praying; but, being conscious of necessities not covered and realms of good not reached, he covered these impenetrable and undiscovered regions by this general plea:

> *Unto him that is able to do exceeding abundantly above all that we ask or think, according to the power that worketh in us.* (Eph. 3:20)

The promise is, "Call unto me, and I will answer thee, and show thee great and mighty things, which thou knowest not" (Jer. 33:3).

James declared that "the effectual fervent prayer of a righteous man availeth much" (James 5:16). There was much that he could not put into words, but he illustrated the idea by the power of Old Testament praying. In this way, he stirred up New Testament saints to imitate, by the fervor and influence of their praying, the holy men of old, and to duplicate and surpass the power of their praying. Elijah, said James,

> *was a man subject to like passions as we are, and he prayed earnestly that it might not rain: and it rained not on the earth by the space of three years and six months. And he prayed again, and the heaven gave rain, and the earth brought forth her fruit.* (James 5:17-18)

In the Revelation of John, the whole lower order of God's creation and His providential government, the church and the angelic world, are in an attitude of waiting. They are waiting for the efficiency of the prayers of the saints on earth to carry out the various interests of earth and heaven. The angel takes the fire kindled by prayer and casts it earthward, "and there were voices, and thunderings, and lightings, and an earthquake" (Rev. 8:5). Prayer is the force that creates all these alarms, disturbances, and struggles. "Ask of me," says God to His Son, and to the church of His Son, "and I shall give thee the heathen for thine inheritance, and the uttermost parts of the earth for thy possession" (Ps. 2:8).

The men who have done mighty things for God have always been mighty in prayer, have well understood the possibilities of prayer, and have made the most of these possibilities. The Son of God, the first of all and the mightiest of all, has shown us the all-powerful and far-reaching possibilities of prayer. Paul was mighty for God because he knew how to use, and how to get others to use, the mighty spiritual forces of prayer.

The seraphim, burning, sleepless, adoring, is the emblem of prayer. (See Isaiah 6:1–7.) It is resistless in its ardor, devoted and tireless. There are hindrances to prayer that nothing but pure, intense flame can surmount. There are toils and outlays and endurance that nothing but the strongest, most ardent flame can withstand. Prayer may be low-tongued, but it cannot be cold-tongued. Its words may be few, but they must be on fire. Its feelings may not be impetuous, but they must be white with heat. It is the "effectual fervent prayer" (James 5:16) that influences God.

When prayer fails, the world prevails. When prayer fails, the church loses its divine characteristics, its divine power; the church is swallowed up by a proud ecclesiasticism, and the world scoffs at its obvious impotence.

God's house is the house of prayer (see Isaiah 56:7); God's work is the work of prayer. It is the zeal for God's house (see Psalm 69:9) and the zeal for God's work that make God's house glorious and His work abide.

Chapter 10

Prayerless
Praying

We ought to give ourselves to God with regard to things both temporal and spiritual, and seek our satisfaction only in the fulfilling of His will, whether He leads us by suffering, or by consolation, for all would be equal to a soul truly resigned. Prayer is nothing else but a sense of God's presence. —Brother Lawrence

Why do we not pray? What are the hindrances to prayer? These are not curious or trivial questions. They reach not only to the whole matter of our praying, but also to the whole matter of our religion. Religion is bound to decline when praying is hindered. That which hinders praying, hinders religion. He who is too busy to pray will be too busy to live a holy life.

Other duties often become pressing and absorbing and crowd out prayer. If an inquest could be secured on this dire, spiritual calamity, the coroner's verdict, in many cases of dead praying, would be, "Choked to death." This way of hindering prayer has become so natural, so easy, so innocent, that it comes on us without warning. If we will once allow our praying to be crowded out, it will always be crowded out.

More than anything else, Satan wants us to let the grass grow on the path to our prayer chamber. A vacant chamber of prayer means that a believer has gone out of business religiously, or, what is worse, has made a change and is carrying out our religion in some other name than God's and to somebody else's glory. In the business of religion, God's glory is only secured when we practice that religion with a large capital of prayer.

The apostles understood this when they declared that their time must not be employed in even the sacred duties of almsgiving; they must give themselves, they said, "continually to prayer, and to the ministry of the word" (Acts 6:4); prayer was put first with them, and the ministry of the Word derived its efficiency and life from prayer.

The process of hindering prayer by crowding it out is simple and goes in stages, one after the other. First, one hurries through prayer. Unrest and agitation, which are fatal to all devout exercises, come in. Then the time one spends at prayer is shortened, while one's inclination for the exercise dwindles. Then prayer is crowded into a corner and depends on fragments of time for its exercise. Its value depreciates. By this point, the duty has lost its importance. It no longer commands respect or brings any benefit. It has fallen out of esteem, out of the heart, out of the habits, out of the life. When one ceases to pray, he ceases to live spiritually.

There is no defense against the desolating floods of worldliness and business and cares, except prayer. Christ meant this when He charged us to "watch and pray" (Matt. 26:41). There is no pioneering corps for the Gospel except prayer. Paul knew this when he declared that "night and day [we pray] exceedingly that we might see your face, and might perfect that which is lacking in your faith" (1 Thess. 3:10). There is no arriving at a high state of grace without much praying, and there is no staying in those high altitudes without great praying. Epaphras knew this when he labored "fervently...in prayers" for the Colossian church, "that [they might] stand perfect and complete in all the will of God" (Col. 4:12).

The only way to preserve our praying from being hindered is to regard prayer at its true and high value. We must esteem it as Daniel did, who,

> *when* [he] *knew that the writing was signed, he went into his house; and his windows being opened in his chamber toward Jerusalem, he kneeled upon his knees three times a day, and prayed, and gave thanks before his God, as he did aforetime.* (Dan. 6:10)

Set a high value on praying, as Daniel did, above prestige, honor, leisure, wealth, or life. Make praying one of your habits, as Daniel did. The phrase *as he did aforetime* has much in it to give firmness and fidelity in the hour of trial, much in it to remove hindrances and to master opposing circumstances.

One of Satan's wiliest tricks is to destroy the best by the good. Business and other duties are good, but we are so filled with these that they crowd out and destroy the best. Prayer holds the citadel for God; and if Satan can by any means weaken prayer, he has succeeded so far. When prayer is dead, the citadel is taken. We must keep prayer in the same way that the faithful sentinel keeps guard—with sleepless vigilance. We must not keep it half-starved and feeble as a baby, but we must keep it in giant strength. Our prayer chamber should have our freshest strength, our calmest time; its hours should be unfettered, without intrusion, without haste.

Having a private place and plenty of time in which to pray, is the life of prayer. To kneel upon our knees three times a day and pray and give thanks before God as we did aforetime (see Daniel 6:10), is the very heart and soul of religion, and makes men, like Daniel, of "an excellent spirit" (Dan. 5:12; 6:3), "greatly beloved" (Dan. 10:11) in heaven.

The greatness of prayer, in the most intense form, is not realized without spiritual discipline, because it involves the whole man. Richard Cecil has said, "Prayer is faith passing into act—a union of the will and intellect being realized in an intellectual act. It is the whole man that prays. Less than this is wishing or lip service, a sham or a mummery." This makes prayer hard work; and before this exacting and consuming effort, our spiritual sloth or feebleness stands abashed.

The simplicity of prayer and its childlike elements also form a great obstacle to true praying. Intellect gets in the way of the heart. Only the childlike spirit is the spirit of prayer, and it is no easy task to make the man a child again. In song, in poetry, in memory he may wish himself a child again, but in prayer he must be a child again in reality—just as he was at his mother's knee: artless, sweet, intense, direct, trustful; with no shade of doubt, no temper to be denied. He must have a desire that burns and consumes, that can only be voiced by a cry. It is not easy work to have this childlike spirit of prayer.

If meant spending only one hour in prayer each day, difficulties would confront and hinder even that hour; but praying is keeping one's whole life in preparation for the prayer closet. How difficult it is to cover home and business, all the sweets and all the bitters of life, with the holy atmosphere of the prayer closet! A holy life is the only preparation for prayer. It is just as difficult to pray as it is to live a holy life.

In this fact we find the reason why a wall of exclusion is built around our prayer closets: men do not love holy praying because they do not love and because they do not determine to live holy lives. Montgomery set forth the difficulties of true praying when he declared the sublimity and simplicity of prayer:

> Prayer is the simplest form of speech
> That infant lips can try.

> Prayer is the sublimest strains that reach
> The Majesty on high.

This is not only good poetry, but a profound truth as to the loftiness and simplicity of prayer. There are great difficulties in reaching the exalted, angelic strains of prayer. The difficulty of coming down to the simplicity of infant lips is not much less.

Prayer in the Old Testament is called wrestling. Conflict and skill and strenuous, exhaustive effort are involved. In the New Testament we have the terms *striving, laboring fervently, fervent, effectual, agony,* all indicating that when intense effort is put forth, difficulties are overcome. We, in our praises, sing out—

> What various hindrances we meet
> In coming to a mercy seat.

We have also learned that the gracious results secured by prayer are generally proportional to the effort we put forth in removing the hindrances that obstruct our soul's high communion with God.

Christ said, "Men ought always to pray, and not to faint" (Luke 18:1), and He gave us a parable to illustrate this. The parable of the importunate widow teaches the difficulties in praying, how they are to be surmounted, and the happy results that follow from valorous praying. Difficulties will always obstruct the way to the prayer closet as long as it remains true

> That Satan trembles when he sees
> The weakest saint upon his knees.

Courageous faith is made stronger and purer when it masters difficulties. These difficulties simply focus the eye of faith on the glorious prize that is to be won by the successful wrestler in prayer. (See 1 Corinthians 9:24.) Men must not faint in the contest of prayer, but to this high and holy work they must give themselves, defying the difficulties in the way, and thereby experiencing more than an angel's happiness in the results. Luther said, "To have prayed well is to have studied well." More than that, to have prayed well is to have fought well; to have prayed well is to have lived well; to pray well is to die well.

Prayer is a rare gift, not a popular, ready gift. Prayer is not the fruit of natural talents; rather, it is the product of faith, of holiness, of deeply spiritual character. Men learn to pray as they learn to love, for, as Fénelon said, "Perfect prayer is only another name for love." Perfection in simplicity, in humility, in faith— these form its chief ingredients. Novices in these graces cannot be experts in prayer. It cannot be seized upon by untrained hands; only graduates in heaven's highest school of art can touch its finest keys, raise its sweetest, highest notes. For to graduate from the school of prayer is to master the whole course of a religious life. Fine material, fine finish are requisite. Master workmen are required, for mere journeymen cannot execute the work of prayer.

The spirit of prayer should rule our spirits and our conduct. The spirit of the prayer chamber must control our lives, or the hour in the prayer closet will be dull and sapless. Always praying in our spirits, always acting in the spirit of praying—these make our praying strong. The spirit of every moment is that which imparts strength to the communion of the prayer closet. It is what we are outside of the prayer closet that gives victory or brings defeat to the prayer closet. If the spirit of the world prevails in our non-closet hours, the spirit of the world will prevail in our closet hours, and that will be a vain and idle farce.

We must live for God out of the prayer closet if we want to meet God in the prayer closet. We must bless God with praying lives if we want to have God's blessing in the prayer closet. We must do God's will in our lives if we want to have God's ear in the prayer closet. We must listen to God's voice in public if we want God to listen to our voice in private. God must have our hearts out of the prayer closet if we want to have God's presence in the prayer closet. If we want to have God in the prayer closet, God must have us out of the prayer closet. There is no way of praying to God, except by living to God. The prayer closet is not a confessional, simply, but the hour of holy communion, of high and sweet communication, and of intense intercession.

Men would pray better if they lived better. They would get more from God if they lived more obediently and with the intention to please God. We would have more strength and time for the divine work of intercession if we did not have to expend so much strength and time settling old scores and paying our delinquent taxes. Our spiritual liabilities are so greatly in excess of our spiritual assets that our time in the prayer chamber is spent in filing claims for bankruptcy instead of being a time of great spiritual wealth for us and for others. Our prayer closets are too much like the sign that says, "Closed for Repairs."

John said regarding the praying of the first Christians: "Whatsoever we ask, we receive of him, because we keep his commandments, and do those things that are pleasing in his sight" (1 John 3:22). We should note what measureless grounds were covered, what measureless gifts were received, by their strong praying. "Whatsoever"—how comprehensive is the range and reception of mighty praying, how suggestive of the reasons for the ability to pray and to have prayers answered! Theirs was obedience, but more than mere obedience; they were doing the things that please God well.

They went to their prayer closets, having been made strong by strict obedience and loving fidelity to God in their conduct. Their lives were not only true and obedient, but they were thinking about things above obedience, searching for and doing things to make God glad. This sort of Christian can come with eager step and radiant countenance to meet his Father in the prayer chamber, not simply to be forgiven, but to be approved and to receive.

It makes much difference whether we come to God as a criminal or a child; to be pardoned or to be approved; to settle scores or to be embraced; for punishment or for favor. Our praying, to be strong, must be buttressed by holy living. The name of Christ must be honored by our lives before it will honor our intercessions. The life of faith perfects the prayer of faith.

Our lives not only give color to our praying, but they give body to it as well. Bad living leads inevitably to bad praying, and we pray feebly because we live feebly. The stream of praying cannot rise higher than the fountain of living. The force of the prayer closet is made up of the energy that flows from the confluent streams of living. Therefore, any feebleness of living will throw its faintness into our prayer chambers. We cannot talk to God strongly when we have not lived for God strongly. The prayer closet cannot be made holy to God when the life has not been holy to God. Note that the Word of God emphasizes how our conduct affects the value of our praying:

> *Then shalt thou call, and the LORD shall answer; thou shalt cry, and he shall say, Here I am. If thou take away from the midst of thee the yoke, the putting forth of the finger, and speaking vanity.*
>
> *(Isa. 58:9)*

Men are to pray, "lifting up holy hands, without wrath and doubting" (1 Tim. 2:8). We are to pass the time of our sojourning here in the fear of the Lord if we wish to call on the Father. We cannot divorce praying from conduct. "Whatsoever we ask, we receive of him, because we keep his commandments, and do those things that are pleasing in his sight" (1 John 3:22). "Ye ask, and receive not, because ye ask amiss, that ye may consume it upon your lusts" (James 4:3). The injunction of Christ, "Watch and pray" (Matt. 26:41), is to cover and guard our conduct, that we may come to our prayer closets with all the force secured by a vigilant guard over our lives.

Our religion breaks down most often and most sadly in our conduct. Beautiful theories are marred by ugly lives. The most difficult, as well as the most impressive, point in piety is to live it. Our praying suffers from bad living as much as our religion does. Preachers were charged in earlier times to preach by their lives or to not preach at all. So Christians everywhere ought to be charged to pray by their lives or to not pray at all.

Of course, the prayer of repentance is acceptable; but repentance means to quit doing wrong and learn to do well. A repentance that does not produce a change in conduct is a sham. Praying that does not result in pure conduct is a delusion; it is prayerless.

We have missed the whole office and virtue of praying if it does not rectify our conduct. The very nature of things is that we must either quit praying or quit bad conduct. Cold, dead praying may exist with bad conduct, but cold, dead praying is no praying in God's eyes. Our praying advances in power as it rectifies our lives. A life growing in its purity and devotion will be a more prayerful life.

The pity is that so much of our praying is without an objective or aim. It is without purpose. How much praying there is by men and women who never abide in Christ—hasty praying, sweet praying full of sentiment, pleasing praying, but not backed by a life wedded to Christ! Popular praying! How much of this praying is from unsanctified hearts and unhallowed lips!

For many people, prayers spring into life under the influence of some great excitement, by some pressing emergency, through some popular clamor, or because of some great peril. However, the conditions of prayer are not there. We rush into God's presence and try to link Him to our cause, inflame Him with our passions, move Him by our peril; but all things are to be prayed for with clean hands, with absolute deference to God's will, and by abiding in Christ. Otherwise, our prayers are prayerless.

Prayerless praying by lips and hearts untrained in prayer, by lives out of harmony with Jesus Christ; prayerless praying, which has the form and motion of prayer but is without the true heart of prayer, never moves God to an answer. It is of such praying that James said: "Ye have not, because ye ask not. Ye ask, and receive not, because ye ask amiss" (James 4:2–3).

The two great evils—not asking, and asking in a wrong way. Perhaps the greater evil is wrong asking, for it has in it the show of duty done, of praying when there has been no praying—a deceit, a fraud, a sham. The times of the most praying are not really the times of the best praying. The Pharisees prayed much, but they were actuated by vanity; their praying was the symbol of their hypocrisy, by which they made God's house of prayer a den of robbers (Matt. 21:13). Theirs were the prayers of state occasions—mechanical, perfunctory, professional, beautiful in words, fragrant in sentiment, well ordered, well received by the ears that heard, but utterly devoid of every element of real prayer. They acted as formalists, described in the following words from Charles Spurgeon:

> A mere formalist can always pray so as to please himself. What has he to do but to open his book and read the prescribed words, or bow his knee and repeat such phrases as suggest themselves

to his memory or his fancy? Like the
Tartarian Praying Machine, give but the
wind and the wheel, and the business is
fully arranged. So much knee-bending
and talking, and the prayer is done. The
formalist's prayers are always good, or,
rather, always bad, alike.

"But the living child of God never offers a
prayer that pleases himself," continued Spurgeon. "His standard is above his attainments;
he wonders that God listens to him, and
though he knows he will be heard for Christ's
sake, yet he accounts it a wonderful instance of
condescending mercy that such poor prayers as
his should ever reach the ears of the Lord God
of Sabaoth."[1]

The conditions of prayer are well ordered
and clear: one of the first necessities, if we are
to grasp the infinite possibilities of prayer, is to
get rid of prayerless praying. Prayerless praying is often beautiful in words and in execution; it has the drapery of prayer in rich and
costly form, but it lacks the soul of praying. It
has been said that

there are no possibilities, no necessity for
prayerless praying. A heartless performance, a senseless routine, a dead habit, a

---

[1] Sabaoth: armies, as in Romans 9:29 and James 5:4.

hasty, careless performance, it justifies
nothing. Prayerless praying has no life,
gives no life, is dead, breathes out death.
Not a battle-ax, but a child's toy—for
play, not for service. Prayerless praying
does not come up to the importance and
aims of a recreation. Prayerless praying
is only a weight, an impediment in the
hour of struggle, of intense conflict, a call
to retreat in the moment of battle and
victory.

We must pray, but we fall so easily into
the habit of prayerless service, of merely filling
a program. As Richard Cecil put it, "A man
may pray night and day and deceive himself."

If only men prayed on all occasions and in
every place where they go through the motion!
If only there were holy, inflamed hearts behind
all these beautiful words and gracious forms! If
only there were always uplifted hearts in these
"upstanding" men, who are uttering flawless
but vain words before God! If only there were
always reverent hearts when men on bended
knees are uttering words before God to please
men's ears!

There is nothing that will preserve the life
of prayer—its vigor, sweetness, obligations,
seriousness, and value—so much as a deep
conviction that prayer is an approach to God, a

pleading with God, an asking of God. Reality will then be in it; reverence will then be in the attitude, in the place, and in the air. Faith will draw, kindle, and open. Formality and deadness cannot live in this high and all-serious home of the soul.

Prayerless praying lacks the essential element of true praying; it is not based on desire, and it is devoid of earnestness and faith. Desire burdens the chariot of prayer, and faith drives its wheels. Prayerless praying has no burden, because it has no sense of need; no ardency, because it has none of the vision, strength, or glow of faith. It has no mighty pressure, no holding on to God with the deathless, despairing grasp, "I will not let thee go, except thou bless me" (Gen. 32:26). It has no utter self-abandonment, lost in the throes of a desperate, pertinacious, and consuming plea: "Yet now, if thou wilt forgive their sin—; and if not, blot me, I pray thee, out of thy book" (Exod. 32:32); or, "Give me Scotland, or may I die."

Prayerless praying stakes nothing on the issue, for it has nothing to stake. It comes with empty hands, indeed, but they are listless hands, as well as empty. They have never learned the lesson of empty hands clinging to the Cross; this lesson, to them, has no form or comeliness. (See Isaiah 53:2.)

Prayerless praying has no heart in its praying. The lack of heart deprives praying of its reality, and makes it an empty and unfit vessel. Heart, soul, life must be in our praying; the heavens must feel the force of our crying, and must be brought into oppressed sympathy for our bitter and needy state. A need that oppresses us, and has no relief but in our crying to God, must voice our praying.

Prayerless praying is insincere. It has no honesty at heart. We name in words what we do not want in heart. Our prayers give formal utterance to the things for which our hearts are not only not hungry, but for which they really have no taste.

I once heard an eminent and saintly preacher, now in heaven, speak abruptly and sharply to a congregation that had just risen from prayer, with the question and statement, "What did you pray for? If God should take hold of you and shake you, and demand what you prayed for, you could not tell Him to save your life what the prayer was that has just died from your lips." So it always is, that prayerless praying has neither memory nor heart. A mere form, a heterogeneous mass, an insipid compound, a mixture thrown together for sound and to fill up time, but with neither heart nor aim, is prayerless praying. A dry routine, a dreary drudge, a dull and heavy task, is this prayerless praying.

But prayerless praying is much worse than either task or drudgery. Indeed, it divorces praying from living; it utters its words against the world, but with heart and life runs into the world; it prays for humility, but nurtures pride; prays for self-denial, while indulging the flesh. Nothing exceeds true praying in its gracious results; but it is better not to pray at all than to pray prayerless prayers, for they are but sinning, and the worst of sinning is to sin on our knees.

The prayer habit is a good habit, but prayer done only by force of habit is a very bad habit. This kind of praying is not conditioned after God's order, nor is it generated by God's power. It is not only a waste, a perversion, and a delusion, but it is also a prolific source of unbelief. Prayerless praying gets no results. God is not reached, self is not helped. It is better not to pray at all than to secure no results from praying—better for the one who prays, better for others.

Men hear of the prodigious results that are to be secured by prayer: the matchless good promised in God's Word to prayer. These keen-eyed worldlings, or timid ones of little faith, mark the great discrepancy between the results promised and results realized, and they are led necessarily to doubt the truth and worth of that which is so big in promise and so beggarly in results. Religion and God are dishonored, doubt and unbelief are strengthened, by much asking and no getting.

In contrast to this, what a mighty force prayerful praying is! Real prayer helps God and man. God's kingdom is advanced by it. The greatest good comes to man by it. Prayer can do anything that God can do. The pity is that we do not believe this as we ought, and we do not put it to the test.

Chapter 11

Wonderful Results of Prayer

Do not we rest in our day too much on the arm of flesh? Cannot the same wonders be done now as of old? Do not the eyes of the Lord run to and fro throughout the whole earth still to show Himself strong on behalf of those who put their trust in Him? Oh, that God would give me more practical faith in Him! Where is now the Lord God of Elijah? He is waiting for Elijah to call on Him. —James Gilmour

The preceding chapter closed with the statement that prayer can do anything that God can do. It is a tremendous statement to make, but it is a statement borne out by history and experience. If we are abiding in Christ (and if we abide in Him we are living in obedience to His holy will and can approach God in His name; see John 15:4–11, 16), then there lie open before us the infinite resources of the divine treasure-house.

The man who truly prays gets from God many things denied to the prayerless man. The aim of all real praying is to get the thing prayed for, as the child's cry for bread has for its end the getting of bread. This view removes prayer clean out of the sphere of religious performances. Prayer is not acting a part or going through religious motions. Prayer is neither official nor formal nor ceremonial, but direct, hearty, intense. Prayer is not religious work that must be gone through, and that avails because it is well done. Rather, prayer is the helpless and needy child crying to the compassion of the Father's heart and the bounty and power of the Father's hand. The answer is as sure to come as the Father's heart can be touched and the Father's hand be moved.

The purpose of asking is to receive. The aim of seeking is to find. The goal of knocking is to arouse attention and get in. This is Christ's iterated and reiterated affirmation: the prayer will be answered, without a doubt, and its end will undoubtedly be secured, not by some roundabout way, but by getting the very thing asked for.

The value of prayer does not lie in the number of prayers or the length of prayers; rather, its value is found in the great truth that we are privileged, by our relationship to

God, to unburden our desires and to make our requests known to Him (Phil. 4:6), and that He will relieve by granting our petitions. The child asks because the parent is in the habit of granting the child's requests. Likewise, we, as the children of God, need something, and we need it badly; and so we go to God for it.

Neither the Bible nor the child of God knows anything of that half-infidel declaration that we are to answer our own prayers. God answers prayer. And the heart of faith knows nothing of that specious skepticism that holds back the steps of prayer and chills its ardor by whispering that prayer does not affect God.

D. L. Moody used to tell a story of a little child whose father and mother had died, and who was taken into another family. The first night she asked whether she could pray as she used to do. They said, "Oh, yes!" So she knelt down and prayed as her mother had taught her; and when that was ended, she added a little prayer of her own: "O God, make these people as kind to me as Father and Mother were." Then she paused and looked up, as if expecting the answer, and then added, "Of course you will." How sweetly simple was that little one's faith! She expected God to answer, and, "of course," she got her request. That is the spirit in which God invites us to approach Him.

In contrast to that incident is the story told of the quaint Yorkshire class leader, Daniel Quorm, who was visiting a friend. One morning he came to his friend and said, "I am sorry you have met with such a great disappointment."

"Why, no," said the man, "I have not met with any disappointment."

"Yes," said Daniel, "you were expecting something remarkable today."

"What do you mean?" asked the friend.

"Why, you prayed that you might be kept sweet and gentle all day long. And, by the way things have been going, I see you have been greatly disappointed."

"Oh," said the man, "I thought you meant something particular." Obviously, this man never expected his prayer to be answered, whereas Daniel fully expected God to hear his friend's prayer.

Prayer is mighty in its operations, and God never disappoints those who put their trust and confidence in Him. They may have to wait long for the answer, and they may not live to see it, but the prayer of faith never misses its objective.

Dr. J. Wilbur Chapman told this story:

A friend of mine in Cincinnati had preached his sermon and sank back in his chair, when he felt impelled to make another appeal. A boy at the back of the church lifted his hand. My friend left the pulpit and went down to him, and said, "Tell me about yourself." The boy said, "I live in New York. I am a prodigal. I have disgraced my father's name and broken my mother's heart. I ran away and told them I would never come back until I became a Christian or they brought me home dead." That night there went from Cincinnati a letter telling his father and mother that their boy had turned to God.

Seven days later, in a black-bordered envelope, a reply came, and it read: "My dear boy, when I got the news that you had received Jesus Christ, the sky was overcast; your father was dead." Then the letter went on to tell how the father had prayed for his prodigal boy with his last breath, and concluded, "You are a Christian tonight because your old father would not let you go."

A fourteen-year-old boy was given a task by his father. It so happened that a group of boys came along just then and enticed the boy away with them, and so the work went undone. But the father came home that evening and said, "Frank, did you do the work that I gave you?"

"Yes, sir," said Frank. He told a lie, and his father knew it, but said nothing. It troubled the boy, but he went to bed as usual. Next morning his mother said to him, "Your father did not sleep all last night."

"Why didn't he sleep?" asked Frank.

His mother said, "He spent the whole night praying for you."

This sent the arrow into his heart. He was deeply convicted of his sin, and knew no rest until he got right with God. Long afterward, when the boy became Bishop Warne, he said that his decision for Christ came from his father's prayer that night. He saw his father keeping his lonely and sorrowful vigil praying for his boy, and it broke his heart. He said, "I can never be sufficiently grateful to him for that prayer."

A certain evangelist once began a series of meetings in a little church of about twenty members who were very cold and dead, and much divided. A little prayer meeting was kept up there by two or three women. This man, who was much used of God, said,

I preached, and closed at eight o'clock. There was no one to speak or pray. The next evening one man spoke. The next morning, I rode six miles to a minister's study, and kneeled in prayer. I went back, and said to the little church: "If you can come up with enough money to board me, I will stay until God opens the windows of heaven. God has promised to bless these means, and I believe He will."

Within ten days there were so many anxious souls that I met one hundred and fifty of them at a time in an inquiry meeting, while Christians were praying in another house of worship. Several hundred, I think, were converted. It is safe to believe God.

A mother asked the late John B. Gough to visit her son, in order to win him to Christ. Gough found the young man's mind full of skeptical notions, and impervious to argument. Finally, the young man was asked to pray, just once, for light. He replied, "I do not know anything perfect to whom or to which I could pray."

"How about your mother's love?" said the orator. "Isn't that perfect? Hasn't she always stood by you, and been ready to take you in and care for you, when even your father had really kicked you out?"

The young man, choked with emotion, said, "Yes, sir; that is so."

"Then pray to Love—it will help you. Will you promise?" He promised.

That night the young man prayed in the privacy of his room. He kneeled down, closed his eyes, and, struggling a moment, uttered the words, "O Love." Instantly, as if by a flash of lightning, the old Bible text came to him: "God is love" (1 John 4:8); and he said, brokenly, "O God!" Then came another flash of divine truth, and a voice said, "God so loved the world, that he gave his only begotten Son" (John 3:16)— and there, instantly, he exclaimed, "O Christ, incarnation of most divine love, show me light and truth." It was all over; he was in the light of the most perfect peace. He ran downstairs and told his mother that he was saved. That young man is today an eloquent minister of Jesus Christ.

A water famine was threatened in Hakodate, Japan. Miss Dickerson, of the Methodist Episcopal Girls' School, saw the water supply getting smaller daily, and, in one of the fall months, appealed to the Board in New York for help. There was no money on hand, and nothing was done. Miss Dickerson inquired the cost of putting down an artesian well, but found the expense too great to be undertaken.

On the evening of December 31, when the water was almost exhausted, the teachers and the older pupils met to pray for water, though they had no idea how their prayer was to be answered. A couple of days later, a letter was received in the New York office, and it went something like this: "Philadelphia, January 1. It is six o'clock in the morning of New Year's Day. All the other members of the family are asleep, but I was awakened with a strange impression that someone, somewhere, is in need of money, which the Lord wants me to supply." Enclosed was a check for an amount that just covered the cost of the artesian well and the piping of the water into the school buildings.

A well-known minister once said to me:

I have seen God's hand stretched out to heal among the heathen in as mighty wonder-working power as in apostolic times. I was preaching to two thousand starving orphan girls at Kedgaum, India, at Ramabai's Mukti (salvation) Mission. A swarm of serpents, as venomous and deadly as the reptile that smote Paul, suddenly raided the walled grounds. They were "sent of Satan," said Ramabai, and several of her most beautiful and faithful Christian girls were smitten by them, two of them bitten twice. I saw four of the very flower of her flock in convulsions at once, unconscious and apparently in the agonies of death.

Ramabai believed the Bible with an implicit and obedient faith. There were three of us missionaries there. She said, "We will do just what the Bible says. I want you to minister for their healing according to James 5:14–18." She led the way into the dormitory where her girls were lying in spasms, and we laid our hands upon their heads and prayed, and anointed them with oil in the name of the Lord. Each of them was healed as soon as anointed, and they all sat up and sang with their faces shining. That miracle and marvel among the heathen mightily confirmed the word of the Lord, and was a profound and overpowering proclamation of God.

Some years ago, the record of a wonderful work of grace in connection with one of the stations of the China Inland Mission attracted a good deal of attention. Both the number and spiritual character of the converts had been far greater than at other stations, where the consecration of the missionaries had been just as great as at the more fruitful place.

This rich harvest of souls remained a mystery until Hudson Taylor, on a visit to England, discovered the secret. At the close of one of Mr. Taylor's addresses, a gentleman came forward to make his acquaintance. In the conversation that followed, Mr. Taylor was surprised at the accurate knowledge the man possessed concerning this inland China station. "But how is it," Mr. Taylor asked, "that you are so conversant with the conditions of that work?"

"Oh!" he replied, "the missionary there and I are old college mates. For years we have regularly corresponded; he has sent me names of inquirers and converts, and these I have daily taken to God in prayer."

At last the secret was found! A praying man at home, praying definitely, praying daily, for specific cases among the heathen—that is the real intercessory missionary.

Hudson Taylor himself, as all the world knows, was a man who knew how to pray and whose praying was blessed with fruitful answers. In the story of his life, told by Dr. and Mrs. Howard Taylor, we find page after page aglow with answered prayer. On his way out to China for the first time, in 1853, when he was

only twenty-one years of age, Hudson Taylor
had a definite answer to prayer that was a
great encouragement to his faith. The biogra-
phers set the scene:

> They had just come through the
> Dampier Strait, but were not yet out of
> sight of the islands. Usually a breeze
> would spring up after sunset and last
> until about dawn. The utmost use was
> made of it, but during the day they lay
> still with flapping sails, often drifting
> back and losing a good deal of the ad-
> vantage gained at night.

The story continues in Hudson Taylor's
own words:

> This happened notably on one occa-
> sion when we were in dangerous prox-
> imity to the north of New Guinea.
> Saturday night had brought us to a
> point some thirty miles off the land, and
> during the Sunday morning service,
> which was held on deck, I could not fail
> to see that the captain looked troubled
> and frequently went over to the side of
> the ship. When the service had ended, I
> learned from him the cause. A four-knot
> current was carrying us toward some

sunken reefs, and we were already so near that it seemed improbable that we should get through the afternoon in safety. After dinner, the longboat was put out, and all hands endeavored, without success, to turn the ship's head from the shore.

After standing together on the deck for some time in silence, the captain said to me: "Well, we have done everything that can be done. We can only await the result."

A thought occurred to me, and I replied: "No, there is one thing we have not done yet."

"What is that?" he queried.

"Four of us on board are Christians. Let us each retire to his own cabin, and in agreed prayer ask the Lord to immediately give us a breeze. He can as easily send it now as at sunset."

The captain complied with this proposal. I went and spoke to two of the other men, and after prayer with the carpenter, we all four retired to wait upon God. I had a good but very brief season in prayer, and then felt so satisfied that our request was granted that I could not continue asking, and very soon went up again on deck. The first officer, a godless man, was in charge. I went over and asked him to let down the clews or corners of the mainsail, which had been drawn up in order to lessen the useless flapping of the sail against the rigging.

"What would be the good of that?" he answered roughly.

I told him we had been asking for a wind from God; that it was coming immediately; and we were so near the reef by this time that there was not a minute to lose.

With an oath and a look of contempt, he said he would rather see a wind than hear of it. But while he was speaking, I watched his eye, following it up to the royal, and there, sure enough, the corner of the topmost sail was beginning to tremble in the breeze.

"Don't you see the wind is coming? Look at the royal!" I exclaimed.

"No, it is only a cat's paw," he rejoined, describing a mere puff of wind.

"Cat's paw or not," I cried, "please let down the mainsail and give us the benefit."

This he was not slow to do. In another minute the heavy tread of the men on deck brought up the captain from his cabin to see what was the matter. The breeze had indeed come! In a few minutes we were plowing our way at six or seven knots an hour through the water...and though the wind was sometimes unsteady, we did not altogether lose it until after passing the Pelew Islands.

Thus God encouraged me, before landing on China's shores, to bring every variety of need to Him in prayer, and to expect that He would honor the name of the Lord Jesus and give the help each emergency required.

In an address at Cambridge some time ago,[1] S. D. Gordon told in his own inimitable way the story of a man in his own country, the United States, to illustrate the reality of prayer, and that it is not mere talking. Said Mr. Gordon:

This man came from an old New England family, a bit farther back an English family. He was a giant in size, and a keen man mentally, and a university-trained man. He had gone out West to live, and represented a prominent

---

[1] This address appeared in *The Life of Faith*, April 3, 1912.

district in our House of Congress, answering to your House of Commons. He
was a prominent leader there. He was
reared in a Christian family; but he was
a skeptic, and he used to lecture against
Christianity. He told me he was fond, in
his lectures, of proving, as he thought,
conclusively, that there was no God.
That was the type of his infidelity.

One day, he told me, he was sitting
in the Lower House of Congress. It was
at the time of a presidential election,
when party feelings ran high. One
would have thought that was the last
place where a man would be likely to
think about spiritual things. He said: "I
was sitting in my seat in that crowded
House and that heated atmosphere,
when a feeling came to me that the God
whose existence I thought I could suc-
cessfully disprove, was right above me,
looking down on me, and that He was
displeased with me, and with the things
I was doing. I said to myself, 'This is ri-
diculous, I guess I've been working too
hard. I'll go and get a good meal and
take a long walk and shake myself, and
see if that will take this feeling away.'"

He got his extra meal, took a walk,
and came back to his seat, but he could

not shake the impression that God was there and was displeased with him. He went for a walk, day after day, but could never shake off the feeling. Then he went back to his constituency in his state, he said, to arrange matters there. He had an ambition to be the governor of his state, and his party was the dominant party in the state; and, as far as such things could be judged, he was in the line to become governor there, in one of the most dominant states of our Central West.

But then, he said: "I went home to fix that thing up as far as I could, and to get ready for it. But I had hardly reached home and exchanged greetings, when my wife, who was an earnest Christian woman, said to me that a few of them had made a little covenant of prayer that I might become a Christian." He did not want her to know the experience that he had just been going through, and so he said as carelessly as he could, "When did this thing begin, this praying of yours?" She named the date. Then he did some very quick thinking, and he knew, as he thought back, that it was the same day when that strange impression came to him for the first time.

This man said to me: "I was tremendously shaken. I wanted to be honest. I was perfectly honest in not believing in God, and I thought I was right. But if what she said was true, then merely as a lawyer sifting his evidence in a case, it would be good evidence that there was really something in their prayer. I was terrifically shaken, and wanted to be honest, and did not know what to do. That same night I went to a little Methodist chapel, and if somebody had known how to talk with me, I think I should have accepted Christ that night."

Then he said that the next night he went back again to that chapel, where meetings were being held each night, and there he knelt at the altar, and yielded his great strong will to the will of God. Then he said, "I knew I was to preach," and he is still preaching in a Western state at the time of this writing.

That is half of the story. I also talked with his wife, because I wanted to put the two halves together, and she told me the following. She had been a Christian—what you might call a nominal Christian—which is a strange confusion of terms. Then there came a time when she was led into a full surrender of her life to the Lord Jesus Christ.

Then she said to me, "At once there came a great intensifying of desire that my husband might be a Christian, and we made that little compact to pray for him each day until he became a Christian. That night I was kneeling at my bedside before going to sleep, praying for my husband, praying very earnestly; and then a voice said to me, 'Are you praying for the results that will come if your husband is converted?'"

The little message was so very distinct that she said she was frightened; she had never had such an experience. But she went on praying still more earnestly, and again there came the quiet voice, "Are you praying for the consequences?" And again there was a sense of being startled, frightened. But she still went on praying and wondering what this meant; and a third time the quiet voice came more quietly than ever, as she described it, "Are you praying for the consequences?"

Then she told me that she said with great earnestness, "O God, I am praying for anything You think is good, if only my husband may know You, and become

a true Christian man." She told me that
when that prayer came from her lips,
there instantly came into her heart a
wonderful sense of peace, a great peace
that she could not explain, a
"peace…[that] passeth all understand-
ing" (Phil. 4:7); and from that moment—
it was the very night of the covenant, the
night when her husband had that first
strange experience—the assurance never
left her that he would accept Christ.

But all those weeks she prayed with
the firm assurance that the result was
coming. What were the consequences?
They were of a kind that I think no one
would think small. She was the wife of a
man in a very prominent political position; she was the wife of a man who was
in the line of becoming the first official
of his state, and she officially the first
lady socially of that state, with all the
honor that that social standing would
imply. Now she is the wife of a Methodist preacher, with her home changed
every two or three years, she going from
this place to that—a very different social position—and having a very different income than she would otherwise
have had. Yet I never met a woman who
had more of the wonderful peace of God

in her heart, and of the light of God in her face, than that woman.

And Mr. Gordon's comment on that incident is this:

Now, you can see at once that there was no change in the purpose of God through that prayer. The prayer worked out His purpose; it did not change it. But the woman's surrender gave the opportunity of working out the will that God wanted to work out. If we would give ourselves to Him and learn His will, and use all our strength in learning His will and bending to His will, then we would begin to pray, and there is simply nothing that can resist the tremendous power of the prayer. Oh, for more men who will be simple enough to get in touch with God, and give Him the mastery of their whole lives, and learn His will, and then give themselves, as Jesus gave Himself, to the sacred service of intercession!

To the man or woman who is acquainted with God and who knows how to pray, there is nothing remarkable in the answers that come. They are sure of being heard, since they ask in accordance with what they know to be the mind and the will of God. Dr. William Burt, Bishop of Europe in the Methodist Episcopal Church, when he visited their Boys' School in Vienna, found that, although the year was not up, all available funds had been spent. He hesitated to make a special appeal to his friends in America. He counseled with the teachers. They took the matter to God in earnest and continued prayer, believing that He would grant their request.

Ten days later, Bishop Burt was in Rome, and there came to him a letter from a friend in New York, which read substantially thus: "As I went to my office on Broadway one morning [and the date was the very one on which the teachers were praying], a voice seemed to tell me that you were in need of funds for the Boys' School in Vienna. I very gladly enclose a check for the work." The check was for the amount needed. There had been no human communication between Vienna and New York. But while they were yet speaking, God answered them.

Some time ago there appeared in an English religious weekly the report of an incident narrated by a well-known preacher in the course of an address to children. This preacher was able to vouch for the truth of the story. A child lay sick in a country cottage, and her younger sister heard the doctor say, as he left the house, "Nothing but a miracle can save her." The little girl went to her money box, took out the few coins it contained, and in perfect simplicity of heart went to shop after shop in the village street, asking, "Please, I want to buy a miracle." From each she came away disappointed. Even the local chemist had to say, "My dear, we don't sell miracles here."

But outside his door two men were talking, and had overheard the child's request. One was a great doctor from a London hospital, and he asked her to explain what she wanted. When he understood the need, he hurried with her to the cottage, examined the sick girl, and said to the mother: "It is true—only a miracle can save her, and it must be performed at once." He got his instruments, performed the operation, and the patient's life was saved.

D. L. Moody gave this illustration of the wonderful results of prayer:

> While I was in Edinburgh, a man was pointed out to me by a friend, who said: "That man is chairman of the Edinburgh Infidel Club." I went and sat beside him and said, "My friend, I am glad to see you in our meeting. Are you concerned about your welfare?"

"I do not believe in any hereafter," he replied.

"Well, just get down on your knees and let me pray for you."

"No, I do not believe in prayer."

So I knelt beside him as he sat, and I prayed for him. He made a great deal of sport of it. A year later, I met him again. I took him by the hand and said: "Hasn't God answered my prayer yet?"

"There is no God," he said. "If you believe in one who answers prayer, try your hand on me."

"Well, a great many people are now praying for you, and God's time will come, and I believe you will be saved yet."

Some time afterwards, I got a letter from a leading barrister in Edinburgh telling me that my infidel friend had come to Christ, and that seventeen of his club men had followed his example. I did not know *how* God would answer prayer, but I knew He would answer. Let us come boldly to God.

Robert Louis Stevenson told a vivid story of a storm at sea. The passengers below were greatly alarmed, as the waves dashed over the vessel. At last, one of them, against orders, crept to the deck, and came to the pilot, who was tied with rope to the wheel, which he was turning without flinching. The pilot caught sight of the terror-stricken man, and gave him a reassuring smile. Below went the passenger, and comforted the others by saying, "I have seen the face of the pilot, and he smiled. All is well."

That is how we feel when, through the gateway of prayer, we find our way into the Father's presence. We see His face, and we know that all is well, since His hand is on the helm of events, and "even the winds and the sea obey him" (Matt. 8:27). When we live in fellowship with Him, we come with confidence into His presence, asking in the full confidence of receiving and meeting with the justification of our faith. (See Hebrews 4:16.)

Chapter 12

The Birthplace
of Revival

Let your hearts be much set on revivals of religion. Never forget that the churches have hitherto existed and prospered by revivals; and that if they are to exist and prosper in time to come, it must be by the same cause which has from the first been their glory and defense.
—*Joel Hawks*

It has been said that the history of revivals is the history of religion, and no one can study their history without being impressed with their mighty influence upon the destiny of the race. To look back over the progress of the divine kingdom upon earth is to review revival periods that have come like refreshing showers upon dry and thirsty ground, making the desert to blossom as the rose (Isa. 35:1), and bringing new eras of spiritual life and activity just when the church had fallen under the influence of the apathy of the times, and needed to be aroused to a new sense of her duty and responsibility.

"From one point of view, and that not the least important," wrote Principal Lindsay, in *The Church and the Ministry in the Early Centuries,*

> the history of the church flows on from one time of revival to another; and whether we take the awakenings in the old Catholic, the medieval, or the modern church, these have always been the work of men specially gifted with the power of seeing and declaring the secrets of the deepest Christian life; and the effect of their work has always been proportional to the spiritual receptivity of the generation they have spoken to.

As God, from the beginning, has worked prominently through revivals, there can be no denial of the fact that revivals are a part of the divine plan. The kingdom of our Lord has been advanced in large measure by special seasons of gracious and rapid accomplishment of the work of conversion; and it may be inferred, therefore, that the means through which God has worked in other times will be employed in our time to produce similar results.

"The quiet conversion of one sinner after another, under the ordinary ministry of the Gospel," according to one writer on the subject,

> must always be regarded with feelings of satisfaction and gratitude by the ministers and disciples of Christ; but a periodical manifestation of the simultaneous conversion of thousands is also to be desired, because it affords a visible and impressive demonstration that God has made Jesus, who was rejected and crucified, both Lord and Christ. (See Acts 2:36.) The conversion of many also demonstrates that, in virtue of His divine mediatorship, He has assumed the royal scepter of universal supremacy, and "must reign, till he hath put all enemies under his feet" (1 Cor. 15:25). It is therefore reasonable to expect that, from time to time, He will repeat that which, on the day of Pentecost, formed the conclusive and crowning evidence of His messiahship and sovereignty.
>
> By so doing, He will startle the slumbering souls of careless worldlings, gain the attentive ear of the unconverted,

and, in a remarkable way, break in upon those brilliant dreams of earthly glory, grandeur, wealth, power, and happiness, which the rebellious and God-forgetting multitudes so fondly cherish. Such an outpouring of the Holy Spirit will form at once a demonstrative proof of the completeness and acceptance of His once offering of Himself as a sacrifice for sin (see Hebrews 10:10), and a prophetic pledge of the certainty that He "shall...appear the second time without sin unto salvation" (Heb. 9:28), to "judge the world with righteousness" (Ps. 96:13).

That revivals are to be expected, proceeding as they do from the right use of the appropriate means, is a fact that needs not a little emphasis in these days, when the material is exalted at the expense of the spiritual, and when ethical standards are supposed to be supreme. But a revival is not a miracle. This was powerfully taught by Charles G. Finney. There might, he said, be a miracle among its antecedent causes, or there might not. The apostles employed miracles simply as a means by which they arrested attention to their message, and established its divine authority.

But the miracle was not the revival. The miracle was one thing; the revival that followed it was quite another thing. The revivals in the apostles' days were connected with miracles, but they were not miracles.

All revivals are dependent upon God; but, in revivals, as in other things, He invites and requires the assistance of man, and the full result is obtained when there is cooperation between the divine and the human. In other words, to employ a familiar phrase, "God alone can save the world, but God cannot save the world alone." God and man unite for the task; the response of the Divine Being is invariably in proportion to human effort and desire. Edward Payson has said of this needed desire:

> I do not believe that my desires for a revival were ever half so strong as they ought to be; nor do I see how a minister can help being in a "constant fever" when his Master is dishonored and souls are destroyed in so many ways.

This cooperation, then, being necessary, what is the duty that we, as coworkers with God, are required to undertake? First of all, and most important of all—the point that I particularly desire to emphasize—we must give ourselves to prayer. "Revivals," as Dr. J. Wilbur Chapman has reminded us,

> are born in prayer. When Wesley prayed, England was revived; when Knox prayed, Scotland was refreshed; when the Sunday school teachers of Tannybrook prayed, eleven thousand young people were added to the church in a year. Whole nights of prayer have always been succeeded by whole days of soulwinning.

When D. L. Moody's church in Chicago lay in ashes, he went over to England, in 1872, not to preach, but to listen to others preach while his new church was being built. One Sunday morning he was prevailed upon to preach in a London pulpit. But, somehow, the spiritual atmosphere was lacking. He confessed afterwards that he had never had such a hard time preaching in his life; everything was perfectly dead, and, as he vainly tried to preach, he said to himself, "What a fool I was to consent to preach! I came here to listen, and here I am preaching."

Then the awful thought came to him that he had to preach again that night, and only the fact that he had given the promise to do so kept him faithful to the engagement. But when Mr. Moody entered the pulpit at night, and faced the crowded congregation, he was conscious of a new atmosphere. "The powers of an unseen world seemed to have fallen upon the audience," he said. As he drew near the close of his sermon, he became emboldened to give out an invitation, and as he concluded he said, "If there is a man or woman here who will tonight accept Jesus Christ, please stand up."

At once about five hundred people rose to their feet. Thinking that there must be some mistake, he asked the people to be seated, and then, in order that there might be no possible misunderstanding, he repeated the invitation, couching it in even more definite and difficult terms. Again the same number rose. Still thinking that something must be wrong, Mr. Moody, for the second time, asked the standing men and women to be seated, and then he invited all who really meant to accept Christ to pass into the vestry. Fully five hundred people did as requested, and that was the beginning of a revival in that church and neighborhood, which brought Mr. Moody back from Dublin, a few days later, that he might assist the wonderful work of God.

The sequel, however, must be given, or my purpose in relating the incident will be defeated.

When Mr. Moody preached at the morning service, there was a woman in the congregation who had an invalid sister. On her return home, she told the invalid that the preacher had been a Mr. Moody from Chicago, and on hearing this she turned pale.

"What," she said, "Mr. Moody from Chicago! I read about him some time ago in an American paper, and I have been praying that God would send him to London, and to our church. If I had known he was going to preach this morning, I would have eaten no breakfast. I would have spent the whole time in prayer. Now, sister, go out of the room, lock the door, send me no dinner; no matter who comes, don't let them see me. I am going to spend the whole afternoon and evening in prayer."

And so, while Mr. Moody stood in the pulpit that had been like an ice chamber in the morning, the bedridden saint was holding him up before God; and God, who ever delights to answer prayer, poured out His Spirit in mighty power.

The God of revivals who answered the prayer of His child for Mr. Moody, is willing to hear and to answer the faithful, believing prayers of His people today. Wherever God's conditions are met, there the revival is sure to fall. Professor Thomas Nicholson, of Cornell

University, related an experience he had, on his first circuit, that impresses anew the old lesson of the place of prayer in the work of God.

> There had not been a revival on that circuit in years, and things were not spiritually hopeful. For more than four weeks, I had preached faithfully, visited from house to house, in stores, shops, and out-of-the-way places, and had done everything I could. The fifth Monday night saw many of the official members at lodges, but only a corporal's guard at the church.
>
> From that meeting, I went home, cast down, but not in despair. (See 2 Corinthians 4:8.) I resolved to spend that night in prayer. Locking the door, I took Bible and hymn book and began to inquire more diligently of the Lord, though the meetings had been the subject of hours of earnest prayer. Only God knows the anxiety and the faithful, prayerful study of that night. Near the dawn, a great peace and a full assurance came that God would surely bless the plan that had been decided upon, and a text was chosen that I felt sure was of the Lord. Dropping upon

the bed, I slept about two hours, then rose, hastily breakfasted, and went nine miles to the far side of the circuit to visit some sick people. All day the assurance increased.

Toward night, a pouring rain set in. The roads were heavy, and I reached home, wet, hungry, and a little late, only to find no fire in the church, the lights unlit, and no signs of service. The janitor had concluded that the rain would prevent the service. So I changed the order, rang the bell, and prepared for war. Three young men formed the congregation, but in that "full assurance," I delivered the message that had been prayed out on the preceding night, as earnestly and as fully as if the house had been crowded. I then made a personal appeal to each young man in turn. Two yielded, and they testified before the meeting closed.

Tired from the long day, I went to a sweet rest, and the next morning, rising a little later than usual, I learned that one of the young men was going from store to store throughout the town telling of his wonderful deliverance, and exhorting the people to salvation. Night after night conversions occurred, until, after two weeks, one hundred and forty-four people testified before the church in forty-five minutes. All three points of that circuit saw a blaze of revival that winter, and family after family came into the church, until the membership was more than tripled.

Out of that meeting, one convert became a successful pastor in the Michigan Conference, another became the wife of one of our best pastors, and a third was in the ministry for a number of years, and then went to another denomination, where he is faithful to this day. Probably none of the members ever knew about my night of prayer, but I certainly believe that God somehow does for the man who thus prays, what He does not do for the man who does not pray. And I am certain that "more things are wrought by prayer than this world dreams of."

All the true revivals have been born in prayer. When God's people become so concerned about the state of religion that they lie on their faces day and night in earnest supplication, the blessing will be sure to fall. Through prayer Hannah found her relief. Everywhere the church was backslidden and apostate; its foes were victorious. Hannah gave herself to prayer, and in sorrow she multiplied her praying. She saw a great revival born out of her praying. When the whole nation was oppressed, Samuel, prophet and priest, was born to establish a new line of priesthood, and Hannah's praying warmed into existence a new life for God. Religion revived and flourished everywhere. Though the praying came from a woman's broken heart, God, true to His promise, *Ask of Me,* heard and answered, sending a new day of holy gladness to revive His people.

It is the same all down the ages. Every revival of which we have any record has been bathed in prayer. Take, for example, the wonderful revival in Shotts, Scotland, in 1630. It was during this time that it became known that several of the then persecuted ministers were to take part in a solemn convocation. As a result, a vast gathering of godly persons assembled on this occasion from all quarters of the country, and several days were spent in joint prayer, in preparation for the service. In the evening, instead of retiring to rest, the multitude divided themselves into little bands, and spent the whole night in supplication and praise. The following Monday was consecrated to thanksgiving, a practice not then common, and it proved to be one of the great days of the feast.

After much entreaty, John Livingston, chaplain to the Countess of Wigtown, a young man and not ordained, agreed to preach to this congregation. He had spent the night in prayer and conference; but as the hour of assembling approached, his heart quailed at the thought of addressing so many aged and experienced saints, and he actually fled from the duty he had undertaken.

But just as the church of Shotts was vanishing from his view, the following words were borne in upon his mind with such a force that he was compelled to return to the work: "Was I ever a barren wilderness or a land of darkness?" (See Jeremiah 2:31.) He took for his text Ezekiel 36:25–26, and discoursed with great power for about two hours. Five hundred conversions were believed to have occurred as a result of that one sermon, thus prefaced by prayer. And this was the report of that revival: "It was the sowing of a seed through Clydesdale, so that many of the most eminent Christians of that country [Scotland] could date their conversion, or some remarkable confirmation of their case, from that day."

Of Richard Baxter[1] it has been said that "he stained his study walls with praying

---

[1] Richard Baxter (1615–1691): English Puritan scholar and writer.

breath; and after becoming thus anointed with the unction of the Holy Ghost, he sent a river of living water over Kidderminster."

Whitefield[2] once prayed, "O Lord, give me souls or take my soul." It has been said that, after much closet pleading, "he once went to the Devil's fair and took more than a thousand souls out of the paw of the lion in a single day."

Charles Finney has said:

> I once knew a minister who had a revival fourteen winters in succession. I did not know how to account for it until I saw one of his members get up in a prayer meeting and make a confession. "Fellow believers," he said, "I have long been in the habit of praying every Saturday night till after midnight for the descent of the Holy Ghost among us. And now [and he began to weep], I confess that I have neglected it for two or three weeks." The secret was out. That minister had a praying church.

H. C. Fish has told the following account of how the prayers of one man brought about a revival:

---

[2] Whitefield: George Whitefield (1714–1770), English Methodist revivalist.

An aged saint once came to the pastor at night and said: "We are about to have a revival." He was asked why he knew so. His answer was, "I went into the stable to take care of my cattle two hours ago, and there the Lord has kept me in prayer until just now. And I feel that we are going to be revived." It was the commencement of a revival.

And so we might go on multiplying illustration upon illustration to show the place of prayer in revival and to demonstrate that every mighty movement of the Spirit of God has had its source in the prayer chamber. The lesson of it all is this, that as workers together with God, we must regard ourselves as in not a little measure responsible for the conditions that prevail around us today. Are we concerned about the coldness of the church? Do we grieve over the lack of conversions? Do our souls go out to God in midnight cries for the outpouring of His Spirit? If not, part of the blame lies at our door. If we will do our part, God will do His.

Little prayer is the characteristic of a backslidden age and of a backslidden church. Whenever there is little praying in the pulpit or in the pew, spiritual bankruptcy is imminent and inevitable. Around us is a world lost in sin, above us is a God willing and able to save. It is our duty to build the bridge that links heaven and earth, and prayer is the mighty instrument that does the work.

Charles Spurgeon has said: "If any minister can be satisfied without conversions, he shall have no conversions." And so the old cry comes to us with insistent voice: "Pray, brethren, pray."

Chapter 13

Our Passport to Assurance

An hour of solitude passed in sincere and earnest prayer, or the conflict with and conquest over a single passion or subtle bosom sin, will teach us more of thought, will more effectually awaken the faculty and form the habit of reflection, than a year's study in the schools without these.   *—Coleridge*

The example of our Lord in the matter of prayer is one that His followers might do well to copy. Christ prayed much, and He taught much about prayer. His life and His works, as well as His teaching, are illustrations of the nature and necessity of prayer. He lived and worked to answer prayer. But the necessity of importunity in prayer was the point He emphasized in His teaching about prayer. He taught not only that men must pray, but that they must persevere in prayer. For, as Robert Hall has said, "the prayer of faith is the only power in the universe to which the great Jehovah yields. Prayer is the sovereign remedy."

In both command and precept, Christ taught us to have energy and earnestness in praying. He also provided us with specific steps, aiding our efforts toward their climax, which is the answering of our prayers. We are to ask, but to the asking we must add seeking, and seeking must pass into the full force of effort in knocking. "Strive and endeavor to pray," one man has said, "even when thou thinkest thou canst not pray:" We must put forth the effort to pray.

The pleading soul must be aroused to effort by God's silence. Denial, instead of abating or abashing, must arouse the soul's latent energies and kindle anew its highest ardor.

In the Sermon on the Mount, in which Christ lays down the cardinal duties of His religion, He not only gives prominence to prayer in general and secret prayer in particular, but He also sets apart a distinct and different section to give weight to importunate prayer. To prevent any discouragement in praying, He lays down as a basic principle the fact of God's great fatherly willingness—that God's willingness to answer our prayers exceeds our willingness to give good and necessary things to our children, just as far as God's ability, goodness, and perfection exceed our infirmities and evil.

As a further assurance and stimulant to prayer, Christ gives the most positive and iterated assurance of answer to prayers. He declares: "Ask, and it shall be given you; seek, and ye shall find; knock, and it shall be opened unto you" (Matt. 7:7). And to make assurance doubly sure, He adds: "For every one that asketh, receiveth; and he that seeketh findeth; and to him that knocketh it shall be opened" (v. 8).

Why does He unfold to us the Father's loving readiness to answer the prayers of His children? Why does He affirm so strongly that prayer will be answered? Why does He repeat that positive affirmation six times? Why does Christ, on two distinct occasions, go over the same strong promises, iterations, and reiterations in regard to the certainty of prayer being answered? Because He knew that there would be delay in many an answer, which would call for importunate pressing, and that if our faith did not have the strongest assurance of God's willingness to answer, delay would break it down.

He also knew that our spiritual sloth would come in, under the guise of submission, and say it is not God's will to give what we ask, and so we would cease praying and lose our case. After Christ had put in a very clear and strong light God's willingness to answer prayer, He then urged us to importunity, and He emphasized that every unanswered prayer, instead of abating our pressure, should only increase our intensity and energy. If asking does not obtain the answer, let asking pass into the settled attitude and spirit of seeking. If seeking does not secure the answer, let seeking pass on to the more energetic and clamorous plea of knocking. We must persevere until we get it. There will be no failure here if our faith does not break down.

But let me clarify my meaning with the words of J. Kennedy Maclean:

> I do not mean that every prayer we offer is answered exactly as we desire it to be. Were this the case, it would mean that we would be dictating to God, and prayer would degenerate into a mere system of begging. Just as an earthly father knows what is best for his children's welfare, so does God take into consideration the particular needs of His human family, and meets them out of His wonderful storehouse. If our petitions are in accordance with His will,

and if we seek His glory in the asking, the answers will come in ways that will astonish us and fill our hearts with songs of thanksgiving. God is a rich and bountiful Father, and He does not forget His children, nor withhold from them anything that it would be to their advantage to receive.

As our great example in prayer, our Lord presents love as a primary condition—a love that has purified the heart from all the elements of hate, revenge, and ill will. Love, or a life inspired by love, is the supreme condition of prayer. Recall that Fénelon said, "Perfect prayer is only another name for love." The thirteenth chapter of 1 Corinthians is the law of prayer as well as the law of love. The law of love is the law of prayer, and to master this chapter from Paul's epistle is to learn the first and fullest condition of prayer.

Christ taught us also to approach the Father in His name. That is our passport. It is in His name that we are to make our petitions known.

Verily, verily, I say unto you, He that believeth on me, the works that I do shall he do also; and greater works than these shall he do; because I go unto my Father.

*And whatsoever ye shall ask in my name,
that will I do, that the Father may be glo-
rified in the Son. If ye shall ask any thing
in my name, I will do it. (John 14:12–14)*

How wide and comprehensive is that
"whatsoever." There is no limit to the power of
that name. "Whatsoever ye shall ask." That is
the divine declaration, and it opens up to every
praying child a vista of infinite resource and
possibility.

And that is our heritage. The relationship
of God and the Son is an eternal relationship of
a Father to His Son. It is also a relationship of
asking and giving—the Son always asking, the
Father always giving. There is also a relationship between Christ and His people. All that
Christ has may become ours if we obey the
conditions. The one secret is prayer. The place
of revealing and of equipment, of grace and of
power, is the prayer chamber; and as we meet
there with God, we will not only win our triumphs, but we will also grow in the likeness of
our Lord and become His living witnesses to
men.

Without prayer, the Christian life, robbed
of its sweetness and its beauty, becomes cold
and formal and dead; but when rooted in the
secret place where God meets and walks and

talks with His own, it will grow into such a testimony of divine power that all men will feel its influence and be touched by the warmth of its love. Thus, resembling our Lord and Master, we will be used for the glory of God and the salvation of our fellow men.

And that, surely, is the purpose of all real prayer and the goal of all true service.

About the Author

Edward McKendree Bounds was born in Shelby County, Missouri, on August 15, 1835, and died August 24, 1913, in Washington, Georgia. He received a public school education at Shelbyville and was admitted to the bar soon after he reached adulthood. He practiced law until called to preach the Gospel at the age of twenty-four.

His first pastorate was in the Monticello, Missouri, circuit. It was while he was serving as pastor in Brunswick, Missouri, that the Civil War began. The young minister was made a prisoner of war because he would not take the oath of allegiance to the federal government. He was sent to St. Louis and later transferred to Memphis, Tennessee.

Finally securing his release, Bounds traveled on foot nearly one hundred miles to join General Pierce's command in Mississippi and was soon after made chaplain of the Fifth Missouri Regiment, a position he held until near the close of the war, when he was captured and held as prisoner at Nashville, Tennessee.

After the war, Bounds was pastor of churches in Tennessee and Alabama. In 1875 he was assigned to St. Paul Methodist Church in St. Louis, where he served for four years. After filling several other pastorates, he was sent to the First Methodist Church in St. Louis, Missouri, for one year and again to St. Paul Methodist Church for three years. At the end of his pastoral career, he became the editor of the *St. Louis Christian Advocate*.

In 1876, in Eufaula, Alabama, he married Emma Elizabeth Barnett, who died ten years later. In 1887 he married Emma's cousin, Harriet Elizabeth Barnett, who survived him. The family included five children, as well as two daughters from his first marriage.

He was a forceful writer and a very deep thinker. He spent the last seventeen years of his life with his family in Washington, Georgia. Most of the time he was reading, writing, and praying. He arose at four o'clock each morning for many years and was indefatigable in his study of the Bible. His writings were read by thousands of people and were in demand by people of every Protestant denomination.

Bounds was the embodiment of humility, with an angelic devotion to Jesus Christ. He reached that high place where self is forgotten and the love of God and humanity is the all-absorbing thought and purpose.

When he was seventy-six years of age, he came to visit me in Brooklyn, New York, and he was so intense that he awoke me and my family at three o'clock in the morning, praying and weeping over the lost of the earth. All during the day he would go into the church next door and be found on his knees until he was called for his meals. This is what he called the "business of praying."

H. W. HODGE